D0507896

CONTENTS

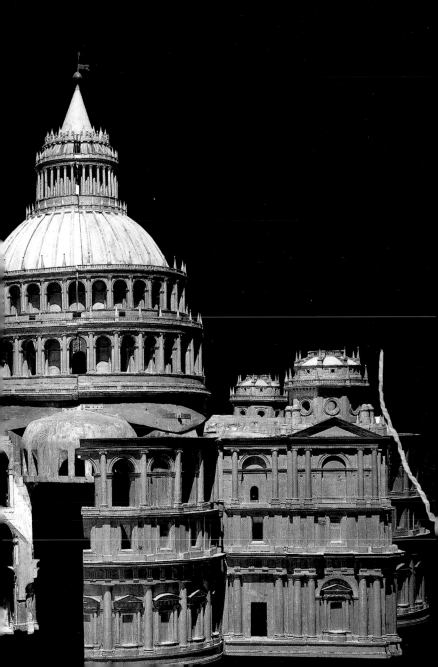

ARCHITECTURE OF THE RENAISSANCE
FROM BRUNELLESCHI
TO PALLADIO

Bertrand Jestaz

THAMES AND HUDSON

The architecture of the Renaissance, inspired by classical antiquity, was born in Italy and spread throughout Europe. It replaced the style that had prevailed during the late Middle Ages, known as Gothic. Seldom has a change been as revolutionary as this one.

CHAPTER 1

THE RETURN TO ANTIQUITY

Although Florence was the city where the Renaissance in art and architecture began, Rome supplied the classical models (left, the Forum by Claude Lorrain) and saw its fullest flowering, with Bramante, Sangallo and Michelangelo. Right: an artist amid ruins.

Gothic art came less naturally to Italy than to France. Churches in Italy, Santa Maria Novella in Florence (left) for example, were less lofty than French churches, and because the builders failed to take advantage of the transfer of weight on to piers in order to open up the walls, they were dark inside. The system of flying buttresses (illustrated below) was seldom used in Italy. The Italians became critical of the pinnacles loading the buttresses, considering such ornament as barbaric or 'Gothic'.

The technical foundations of Gothic architecture

Gothic architecture can be defined by a constructional technique – the pointed rib vault – which determines both its distinctive character and its aesthetic effect. The pointed arch, which is stronger than the round arch, transfers the weight to specific points that are reinforced by buttresses and flying buttresses, and so allows the walls between the load-bearing points to be opened and the lighting of the interior to be improved (and later brought stained-glass windows). Increased verticality encouraged an emphasis on interior height. These two technical advances led to an urge to surpass previous achievements that only spectacular accidents could halt; the basic principles of Gothic architecture, however, were never challenged. The style was the outcome of advances in building techniques that created new criteria of beauty.

The return to style

The Renaissance adopted the opposite approach: style was no longer dependent on technical possibilities but was based on aesthetic principles, on abstract concepts like symmetry and proportion, and on the use of a language that was strictly governed by rules for its vocabulary and syntax – the system of the orders. The Renaissance renounced the exploits of the medieval master-masons, and defined beauty as fidelity to those principles, at the expense of all other considerations; Renaissance architects condemned the Gothic arch and returned to either the round Roman arch, which was considered the purest, or the horizontal architrave, which could be allowed only between two columns. They returned to the barrel vault and to a static view of construction: masonry was made to support only vertically, the load not transferred to unseen buttresses. Weight was seen as weight. A ban was put on showy decoration, excessive height and the elimination of the wall. The insertion of huge windows was also outlawed, resulting in the decline

The taste for classical forms remained alive in Italy and painters used them well before they had become the norm in architecture. In a fresco in San Gimignano (1460, below) Benozzo Gozzoli shows a ciborium (a canopy over an altar) in the new classical style; the ciborium is supported by round arches decorated with flying angels modelled on the winged victories of classical architecture in the spandrels (the triangular space above an arch), and with a classical entablature and frieze containing garlands and ox skulls. The interior is not vaulted but has a flat coffered ceiling.

of the stained-glass window. In this respect architecture took a step back.

The death-sentence of Gothic architecture

The Renaissance condemned the final building style of the Middle Ages out of hand, seeing its manifestations, according to Vasari, as 'hideous and barbaric in their confusion and disorder', as a 'plague of little buildings, one on top of the other', and as an accumulation of decoration 'that removed any sense of proportion from the buildings'. It was said to have been the German barbarians, the Goths 'who had covered Italy with these confounded edifices'; the adjective remained to designate the style. So that they would not repeat such regrettable practices, architects turned to surviving classical monuments to learn the lessons of antiquity.

The interest in Roman art

Paradoxically enough, the return to antiquity originated in Florence, a city that bore no traces of its ancient past, a reminder, perhaps, that art does not depend on opportunity. Brunelleschi and the first Florentines to champion the idea of a renaissance began by studying Romanesque buildings, quite reasonably seeing in them the last vestiges of the principles and forms of ancient art: San Miniato al Monte, with its harmonious façade, and especially the much-loved Baptistry, 'il bel San Giovanni', whose centralized plan, geometrical decoration and mosaics caused it to be classified as classical until the 18th century. This building in fact

Romanesque buildings in Florence, which had retained classical architectural forms, were the earliest source of inspiration. Among these, the façade of San Miniato al Monte (11th century, above) was admired for the harmony of its composition, its round arches, the central feature with its pediment and its geometrical ornament.

provided Francesco della Luna with a justification for the alterations he made to Brunelleschi's façade to the Ospedale degli Innocenti, because it included an example of a moulded architrave turning at right angles to the vertical. Brunelleschi himself, after being defeated by Ghiberti in the competition for the bronze doors of the Baptistry (1401), apparently went off to Rome with Donatello to study ancient monuments, setting the example for what was later to become an essential part of an architect's training.

The Baptistry in Florence (left), on an octagonal centralized plan, was believed to be a classical building. It contained an example of an architrave – the horizontal element – used vertically: an architectural anomaly borrowed on the façade of the Ospedale degli Innocenti (below). Bottom: five of the founding fathers of the Renaissance: Giotto, Uccello, Donatello, Manetti and Brunelleschi.

The antiquities of Rome

A number of monuments still surviving in Rome were to become primary sources for the new architecture. The most influential of all was unquestionably the Pantheon, the only building not in a ruined state because it had been converted into a church, Sancta Maria ad Martyres; it provided the perfect example of the classical pronaos, a portico with large columns supporting a triangular pediment, and also of the perfect central plan, a rotunda covered by a dome.

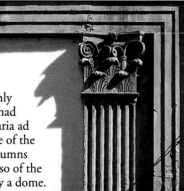

The Forum was the most studied archaeological site in Rome. In the middle of the 17th century Claude Lorrain depicted all the surviving monuments in this classical landscape, seen from the slope of the Capitoline hill. In the foreground on the left, the Arch of Septimius Severus, with above it (thanks to a slight distortion of the perspective) the medieval tower known as the Torre delle Milizie (it is actually further to the left above the Forum of Trajan); next, the portico of the Temple of Antoninus and Faustina, above which can be seen the huge vault of the Basilica of Maxentius (or Constantine); further on is the Colosseum and, to the right, the Arch of Titus still immured in later buildings. The ground is littered with fragments of columns and capitals.

The Colosseum, the Septizonium (a seven-storey building beside the Palatine, only demolished at the end of the 16th century) and, on a less colossal scale, the Theatre of Marcellus, all provided architects with civil examples of a series of orders, one on top of the other. These could also be studied in the remains of the temples in the Forum, but more for the details of capitals and their entablature than for their general proportions as the columns were often partially buried. The arches of Septimius Severus and Titus acted as inspiration for city gates and decorated portals. The baths of Diocletian and Caracalla, gradually excavated during the 16th century, or the Basilica Nova of Maxentius (or Constantine) in the Forum revealed skilful layouts, combining buildings of a variety of shapes in spectacular juxtapositions, and colossal spaces covered with massive vaults. Constantine's basilicas, beginning with Old St Peter's,

The Colosseum (above) provided a perfect model of three storeys of arcades supported by columns belonging to the three orders (Doric, Corinthian, Ionic). The Septizonium (below left), built in the 3rd century AD, was as high as the imperial palace. The arrangement of the orders was studied by artists before the building was demolished by Sixtus V between 1585 and 1590. Hadrian's Pantheon (below), with its centralized plan and its coffered dome, was another ideal model.

which was not demolished until the early 16th century, served to remind people of the nobility of the basilica style, the beauty of the long colonnades in the nave or the atrium. The Roman Campagna and the Via Appia were overflowing with tombs, all built on variations of the central plan. The Eternal City, having been responsible for the initiation of the first Tuscan converts to the Renaissance in the 15th century – Brunelleschi and Giuliano da Sangallo – gradually became the goal of a new type of pilgrimage for architects from Italy (from Bramante to Palladio) as well as abroad (Herrera and Philibert Delorme).

The church of San Lorenzo in Milan provided a unique example of a centrally planned church, surviving intact from ancient times (middle of the 4th century AD). The church partially collapsed in 1573 but was faithfully rebuilt by Martino Bassi.

The antiquities of Italy

By another paradox, the antiquities of southern Italy were not studied in detail, apart from the tombs and villas around Naples, which were drawn by Francesco di Giorgio. The amphitheatre of Capua and the temples of Paestum and Sicily were virtually unknown until the 18th century. In the north, on the other hand, the classical buildings that had survived influenced local styles. In Lombardy San Lorenzo in Milan provided an admirable model of a building with central plan and dome, and a colossal atrium in front. The architects of the Veneto could visit Verona to draw the arena and the triumphal arches, and Pola in Istria for the Arch of the Sergii and the amphitheatre. The Venetians, like the first Florentines, were still sensitive to their pre-Gothic past, Byzantine in their case. Mauro Codussi inherited the 'quincunx' plan (a Greek cross with a large central dome and four minor domes, at each corner) and used it in San Giovanni Crisostomo, with disarming simplicity.

During the Renaissance, architects used the body of the church as a model for centralized structures with a quatrefoil plan, and the chapels attached to three of its four sides as models for octagonal or Greek-cross-shaped structures.

The antiquities of Provence had a direct influence on local building styles in the 16th century. The great gateway of the Château de La Tour d'Aigues (1571, left) has both the general shape and the detailing of a classical triumphal arch. The architect evidently took his inspiration from the arch of the bridge of St Chamas, which still survives.

Roman monuments outside Italy

Antiquities were not confined to Italy, but only those in France received any attention. In Provence the Maison Carrée and the arena in Nîmes, the arena in Arles and the arch and theatre in Orange were studied by Italians who came to draw them. The first to visit the area was Giuliano da Sangallo in about 1495, and Palladio followed later. They influenced local architecture, particularly the high arch in front of the bridge of St Chamas, at the main gateway to the Château de La Tour d'Aigues. The 'piliers de tutelle' (the peristyle of a temple destroyed at the end of the 17th century) in Bordeaux and the gate in Autun were probably admired, but were not studied in detail like the Italian models. There are no known drawings of Roman monuments in Trier or in other German towns. Obviously if architects from north of the Alps felt the need to study classical architecture in the 16th century they preferred to go to Rome, where they could see the most famous ruins of antiquity and the masterpieces of modern architecture.

An unfinished lesson

In this rapid appraisal it is evident that, of all the buildings studied, only the Pantheon, San Lorenzo in Milan and the Christian basilicas survived complete, with an interior as well as an exterior. The others offered either an elevation but no plan (the arches, the arenas and all the surviving columns) or a plan without an elevation (or with a very damaged elevation, like the baths). The artists of the Renaissance had to make a synthesis of the very disparate and incomplete lessons they were learning. In any case, all the monuments were Roman, often very late Roman, never Greek. Their lesson did not include Attic refinements such as optical corrections or sculpture; to them classical antiquity consisted of the scholarly composition and the monumental, or even colossal, scale of the architecture of imperial Rome.

In his views of imaginary classical buildings, Jacques Androuet du Cerceau demonstrates the difficulty experienced by Renaissance architects in visualizing the architecture of antiquity in three dimensions without directly experiencing it. His façades are like screens with nothing behind them, and his Venetian spiral staircase leads nowhere. The use of classical forms, however, for him justifies all such inventions.

& uolenano piu presto saperlo quanti erano cheno · Ancora niuno esacerdoti po
teuano auere una donna · Elli egipti quante uenoleuano & questo faceuano per
re assai gente & non stimauano nessuno bastardo niuni teneuano lignami·

Et ancora dice che uloro figliuoli ghinutricauano amdice derbe · & aderbe · & altre
cose molto uili credo desplagrande moltitudine che erano faceuano ancora exe
citarghi cosacerdoti · & conualeno huomini a imparare scientia · & maxime astro
logia & arismetrica·

EXPLICIT LIBER XX·
INCIPIT LIBER VIGESIMVS PRIMVS·

IN QUESTO VIGESIMO PRIMO LIBRO
strattera daltre cose & dibogni & diuna casa fatta inlu
ogho pantanoso · Perceroto queste sono belle cose chesono i
questo libro doro & buoni ricordi & amaestramenti in
quarda umpoco seue altri edifici pche uinaltra uolta in
tenderemo tutti questi hordini & modi chedice deperco
to sono boghi · Ora uediamo sece altro mausi dornicipre
choqui trata duno casamento ilquale ora muno luogho
pantanoso & aquatio malacqua era salmatra & in
chocchana · dentro ilemare ppiu luoghi sicheghiem molti ar
samenti dogni infralialtri fa mentione solo duno ilquale dice destaua inque
sta forma era lasua misura cento braccia puno uerso & trecento pelaltro il
suo disegnio & forma um ilcorete uedere pcheplu disogniano qui appresso la
quale era inuno quadro diconto braccia · prima doue che uctni braccia er
ducasamenti intorno poi restaua uno chnostro dibraccia sessanta p
non uerso Perintendere bene questo casamento e mestiere chesuneogha pri
ma come sicua ilcasamento ilquado secondo choqui inquesto libro edescrip
to & disegniato cosi io uenanero · Prima come disopra hauete inteso elle
ra trecento braccia plunghezza & larghezza uno quadro diconto
braccia nera sparuto mhabituri come qui sopra uedere lemura dique
sto quadro diconto braccia erano grosse braccia due & questo pche erano
muoltа niune solare & daquello insu erano uno braccia & mezzo pi
sino inmma · Erano queste stanze disoto & cosi disopra larghe braccia sedici
& cosi aneuano ilmuro grosso dentro come disfuori siche ueniua arimanere
uno chnostro dibraccia sessanta doue che inesso sifaceua uno quadro diueti
braccia ilquale aueua lui ancora ilmuro grosso due braccia cheueniua a
rimanere disdici braccia di uacuo doue che intorno intorno acquesto gli
rimaneua spatio diuenti braccia circanarcha donde chediqueste ueni una
cetia dispano cheua intorno acquesto quadro delmezzo sonetoghe tre bra
cia neto intorno intorno secondo ua questo spatio ditre braccia & inordia

One result of the return to the classical style was that the Renaissance submitted to the rules – regularity, symmetry, proportion – that now had to govern all architectural design. These general principles have become so familiar to us that it requires an effort of the imagination to remember that they represented a fundamental break with, and reaction against, the empirical practices of the Middle Ages.

CHAPTER 2
NEW PRINCIPLES

Even before the end of the 15th century, painters liked to depict ideal cities in paintings that are virtually exercises in perspective. The townscape here (right) is arranged around a circular church in the classical manner. Left: project for a *palazzo* by Filarete.

Regular plans

The first and simplest principle was the compulsory return to the use of the ruler, T-square and dividers in the design of buildings. Orthogonal regularity, though sometimes maintained in churches because of the functional constraints of the building, had disappeared from civil architecture, which generally submitted to the requirements of a site. The Renaissance marked a return to precise outlines, rectilinear façades and right-angled corners. Irregular plans, and obtuse or acute angles were outlawed. This did not

In his treatise, written between 1461 and 1464, Filarete proposes geometrical plans that appear too simplistic to be viable (left). The one illustrated here, however, is very similar to his design for the Ospedale Maggiore in Milan (1456), which remained influential for many years.

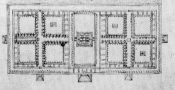

represent any great change in Italy, where the lessons of antiquity had persisted quite strongly throughout the Middle Ages, but it made a noticeable difference in other countries, particularly in France. The buildings erected at Amboise, Blois or Gaillon in about 1550 juxtaposed in a very obvious manner rectangular edifices with much older and irregularly built ones; the resulting mis-match clearly emphasized the difference between the new order and the old empiricism. Very soon the regular plan became obligatory, and this explains why châteaux rebuilt during the second quarter of the 16th century on medieval foundations, like

Regularity of plan and exact right angles were the essential features of the new architecture. At Fontainebleau (below) the part of the palace reconstructed on the medieval foundations (on the right) is easily identifiable. The so-called Oval Court (whose outline is in fact very irregular) is medieval, the later great lower courtyard (on the left) and the Fountain Court (in the centre) are both rectangular.

the first one at Fontainebleau, St-Germain-en-Laye or Chantilly, present an abnormal and quite surprising degree of irregularity. The same problems had to be faced in Germany and can be seen in castles like Heidelberg or Trausnitz in Landshut, or in the Residenz at Munich or Dresden. As a general rule it is probably true to say that instances of non-orthogonal plans in 16th-century buildings are very rare indeed. The circular courtyards in Caprarola, in Italy, or in the Palace of Charles V in Granada might be mentioned as examples, or the pentagonal exterior plan in Caprarola, which was in fact imposed by the outline

Apart from the rectangle, the only acceptable shape was the circle. The courtyard in the Palace of Charles V in the Alhambra in Granada (above) was built to a circular plan by Pedro Machuca, who took his inspiration from Raphael's courtyard in the Villa Madama in Rome.

of the fortress used as its base. It might be stated as a general principle, therefore, that the presence of an oblique wall in a Renaissance building indicates a rebuilt site, or harks back to an earlier layout.

Regular bays

Regularity in the spacing of window bays also became compulsory at this time. This principle was followed to a degree for religious architecture, even if the bays in many Gothic churches are far from regular, but it had been forgotten completely for civil construction. Windows were placed in façades according to the demand for light rather than for the sake of appearance; they were of variable dimensions and the piers between them were of differing widths. Here again Italy had little trouble in returning to good habits. Regularly spaced bays of equal width were created by Brunelleschi in the façade of the Ospedale degli Innocenti, by Michelozzo in the Palazzo Medici and by Alberti in the Palazzo Rucellai (all in Florence) and by the second half of the 15th century the principle had been accepted everywhere. The irregular

Alberti provided the first example of a regularly planned façade in 1455; his windows in the Palazzo Rucellai in Florence are centrally placed within bays defined by pilasters (below). By the time Ammannati came to design the façade on the courtyard of the Palazzo Pitti (left) regularity had become the rule.

façade facing the courtyard of the Doge's Palace in Venice, rebuilt after the fire of 1483, is an anomaly that can only be explained by the fact that old masonry was reused.

The regularity of window size appears to have been the first of the new principles to catch on in France; it was the most necessary and the most superficially successful antidote to empiricism: the Charles VIII wing at Amboise had adopted it already. Nevertheless, it took time for the principle to be applied strictly: it was just beginning to make its appearance at Blois, on the exterior façade of the Louis XII wing and the François I wing. It was imperfectly applied in the Oval Court at Fontainebleau and at Ecouen, and did not really become common practice until the mid-16th century. In fact, until the 17th century, the half-casement windows, which opened out on hinges and should have been banned outright as being incompatible with regular bays, were permitted and were still in use; they can be seen in the north wing of the château at Bonruazel, built in 1585 and in other respects commendably faithful to classicism. Likewise in Germany an effort had to be made to keep to a standard size of window bay, but from the middle of the century on great buildings like the Ott-Heinrichsbau of Heidelberg castle or the Residenz in Landshut began to observe this principle seriously.

Regularity of design was *de rigueur*, even in palaces with no orders, as was often the case in Florence. Below: the model of the Palazzo Strozzi (1489) in which each row of windows is exactly above the one below. Variety and originality could be achieved with the different rustication given to the stone.

Regular window bays, in straight lines, were slow to become the norm outside Italy. In the François I wing at Blois (1515–9, left) the spacing between the bays is irregular and the spiral staircase upsets the line of the storeys.

The alignment of window bays

The regularization of the size of windows inevitably led to their alignment on a single level. Although nowadays this notion seems self-evident, it too had to be re-invented after centuries of empiricism. There was a problem, however, with the lighting of stairways. Traditional spiral staircases were lit by oblique openings that followed the rise of the staircase, as at Chaumont, in the François I wing at Blois or, in about 1535, in Schloss Hartenfels in Torgau. The straight, Italian staircase that replaced these was usually aligned with the perpendicular of the façade; it would need to have a mezzanine between two flights that could only be lit by an opening between two storeys. The result of this was a break in the alignment of the bays, almost universal in French châteaux, which reveals at a glance the position of the staircase: thus at Azay-le-Rideau, Lescot's wing of the Louvre (at the back) and at Assier. Whilst the Italian staircase survived, this anomaly persisted (at Beaumesnil and Cheverny), only ceasing when a spiral staircase, which could be lit at each landing, was adopted. Paradoxically the problem did not arise in Italy because straight staircases were not placed against the façade but in a corner of the courtyard and could therefore be lit from the side, as at Urbino or in the Palazzo Farnese in Rome.

In Italy, on the other hand, regularity and symmetry were accepted without question. Vasari applied the two principles rigorously in his design for the Uffizi in Florence (1560, below), a huge collection of administrative buildings opening on to the Arno at one end.

Symmetry

Concern for regularity led inevitably to a search for symmetry in the modern sense of the word, that is the exact matching of the two halves of a building, on either side of a central axis. In order for the building to be symmetrical, the plan first had to be symmetrical, and this of necessity involved a fundamental rationalization of architectural design. The Italian or Spanish palace, traditionally square with a courtyard, readily submitted to this process. Churches shaped like a Latin cross were already symmetrical but now, with the centralized plan, the temptation to make all axes symmetrical proved irresistible. This was the origin, in fact, of all the variations on the Greek cross that flowered in Renaissance Italy. They provide one of the most attractive chapters in her architectural history.

In France, where very few churches were being built, the design of châteaux was heavily influenced by the notion of symmetry. Gradually the L-shaped plan, widely used in medium-sized houses (Azay-le-Rideau, Villesavin, Fleury-en-Bière, Vallery), was replaced by a two-winged plan like a square U-shape. Symmetry favoured square buildings (Chenonceaux, Chambord, Challeau, La Muette at St-Germain-en-Laye, Ecouen, Ancy-le-Franc), or rectangles (the Château de Madrid in the Bois de Boulogne, the Tuileries). Sebastiano Serlio, who retired to Fontainebleau in 1541, used its plan in his Book VI for all the examples of civil architecture,

In his treatise, Filarete presented his idealized plan for the Ospedale Maggiore in Milan (below, and plan p. 26), which differed from what was actually built. The continuous arcaded loggias provided a horizontal regularity broken only by the vertical pavilions. The central entrance was emphasized by the high staircase leading up to the door (detail far right) rather than by the size of the door itself.

The L-shaped design of Azay-le-Rideau (left), re-built in 1518, at one time also included a short left-hand wing of earlier date and an oblique wall (both now demolished) around an irregular courtyard, the latter constituting an essential feature of the Renaissance dwelling; the asymmetry was accepted. The entrance is not in the centre of the façade but can be distinguished by the tall pavilion that rises above the roof, with irregular windows admitting light to the straight staircase.

whatever their basic geometrical layout. Androuet du Cerceau was undoubtedly inspired by Serlio's writings on architecture, as the similar designs published in his first book in 1559 and in his final one in 1582 testify.

The centrally placed entrance

A symmetrical plan required a median axis. The Italians had remained loyal to the principle of regularity in classical architecture, in which the bays of colonnades are all equal, and so made no particular effort to emphasize the axis. They usually allowed it to pass through the middle of a bay, which had the effect of giving an uneven number of bays. The great

public palaces of Italy, like the Library, the Mint or the Procuratie Nuove in Venice, the Basilica in Vicenza, the Uffizi in Florence and lateral palaces of the Capitoline in Rome, and many private palaces as well (buildings by Bramante and Raphael in Rome, by Sanmicheli in Verona) have façades that are uninterrupted by any particular central feature. In other countries, where the grand church entrance was traditional, the central bay was emphasized by making it a monumental doorway. The French châteaux are a good example. In Blois, built in the reign of Louis XII, the entrance is placed off

In the Palacio de la Cancilleria in Granada (below left) the central entrance is accentuated by the pillars surrounding it. Philibert Delorme designed the portal at Anet in the same way, framing the central bay of the façade with three orders of superimposed columns, and creating a distinctively tall entrance (below). This portal was admired so much that when the rest of the façade was demolished it was saved.

centre. During the reign of François I the median axis prevailed and from 1540 it became conventional to build a projecting bay with superimposed columns, like a sort of modern triumphal arch: these can be seen at Ecouen, Anet and the Louvre. The development of the central element culminated in its transformation into a separate small pavilion standing out from the façade and enhanced with special decorative features (columns, decorative stonework, sculpture) and with a dominant, eye-catching upper part; this remained the standard treatment until the end of the 17th century. In Spain, which took its inspiration more directly from the *palazzi* of Italy, the central entrance was emphasized by a grand entrance with columns (the Palace of Charles V and the Cancilleria in Granada, the Alcazar in Toledo). In Germany, the entrance might be accentuated by heavy decoration but it was not built as a projecting bay, nor as a separate pavilion.

The church of Santo Spirito in Florence is the best example of Brunelleschi's theories. Not only does he echo the classical basilica, with columns down the length of the nave and a

Proportion or calculated harmony

Proportion, or the relationship between dimensions, was one of the overriding concerns of the Renaissance. In the Middle Ages the simplest notion of proportion was entertained, to be applied only to religious architecture, where, at best, some correlation between the height and the breadth of the nave would be attempted, based on a simple geometrical figure such as a square or a triangle. In the Renaissance emphasis was placed on number, precise measurements and harmony, the secret of which, it was believed, could be discovered through arithmetic. Brunelleschi applied himself to the problem at the beginning of the 15th

coffered ceiling, but he bases the plan on a regular square module, and the elevation on a ratio between the height of the arcades and the height of the upper windows. The regularity and harmony of the interior have impressed visitors to the church ever since the Renaissance.

century: the proportions of San Lorenzo were determined by the pre-existing building, but the height of the arches and the nave are in the proportion of 7 to 11; in Santo Spirito, designed entirely by Brunelleschi, the proportions are 6 to 12, which cannot be accidental. It took a real humanist like Alberti to go back to classical theories of harmony and proportion: Pythagoras had worked out that the intervals in music were based on the relationship between lengths (of organ pipes or vibrating strings), and these were in the proportion of 1 to 2 (octave), 2 to 3 (fifth) and 3 to 4 (fourth). In *Timaeus* Plato had deduced that the immanent harmony of the world, revealed in musical concord, was based on the geometrical progression of numbers doubling (1–2–4–8) or trebling (1–3–9–27). Alberti saw these relationships as the means of establishing ideal proportions; architecture would possess the same natural harmony as music, and the idea that the two arts were inter-connected became current in treatises on harmony.

The title page of Gaffurio's treatise on harmony (1518) demonstrates how music and architecture conform to the same laws of proportion. To the right of the author, organ pipes of different lengths express the intervals in music.

To his left, the same intervals, expressed as cords accompanied by a pair of dividers, illustrate their application to architecture.

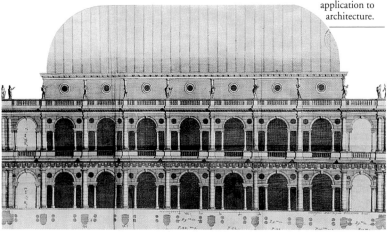

This principle was advocated once again by a Venetian humanist, Francesco di Giorgi, in a design for the construction of the church of San Francesco della Vigna (1535): by basing its dimensions on multiples of 3, all its parts would be in the proportion of fifths or octaves, its length being comparable to an interval of a double octave plus a fifth. Palladio, who studied in the same Venetian milieu, established a relationship between the dimensions that was either arithmetical (6–9–12, for example), or geometrical (4–6–9, 4 being to 6 as 6 is to 9) or harmonic (6–8–12, 6 being separated from 8 by its third, as is 12 from 8). The effectiveness of such sophisticated theory is open to question, or rather our physical ability to perceive such subtle relationships. Yet it did have the merit of pointing the architects of the Renaissance in the direction of the overriding principle of Greek art, commensurability (the 'symmetry' which they had understood in quite a different sense): according to the Greeks, all the dimensions of a monument had to be multiples of a basic module if harmony was to be achieved. Few architects, it is true, were capable of understanding and implementing calculations as learned as those of Palladio, but the idea of modular proportion was in the air, affecting everyone to some extent, consciously or unconsciously, and was bound to encourage them away from empirical solutions.

The architect of the Basilica in Vicenza (opposite bottom), Palladio, was responsible for pushing the theory of proportion and harmony to its limit. Geometry and the theory of proportion had fascinated the humanists for years. Luca Pacioli (below) had become famous through his book *Summa de arithmetica* (1494). Jacopo de' Barbari depicted him in 1495 drawing the figure for one of Euclid's theorems. Beside him on the table are a pair of dividers and a dodecahedron.

The Renaissance in architecture was characterized by forms taken from the art of antiquity. Columns, capitals and entablatures, cupolas, domes and ornament all made up the new vocabulary of the Renaissance style. The orders, at once a system of proportion and of decoration, were the basic structure of the new language.

CHAPTER 3

NEW LANGUAGE

The small church of Sant'Eligio degli Orefici in Rome (right) is a rare example of Raphael's architecture. Its plan is a Greek cross, its basic structure cuboid surmounted by a dome on a drum. Left: a 15th-century detail from *Presentation of the Virgin in the Temple* in a classical setting.

The use of the column in classical architecture

The characteristic element of classical architecture was the column, to which we can assimilate the pilaster, which is simply a column flattened and attached to the wall. The complexity and elegance of the column makes each one a work of art. The shaft is slightly curved to correct the impression of narrowing given by an elongated cylinder. Like a statue, it stands on a pedestal to which it is attached by a moulded base, and is surmounted by a capital. As a vestigial survival of the time when they were built of wood, columns invariably bear a horizontal entablature composed of three elements: an architrave (from the Latin word *architrabs*, main beam), a frieze and a projecting cornice. When a classical building combines arches and columns, like the Colosseum, these are treated as independent systems, juxtaposed without being linked: the arches are supported by pillars and the columns, placed in front of these pillars, support the entablature.

During the Middle Ages the column did not disappear completely, but was reduced to its most basic form: a cylindrical support without curve or proportion, used to carry rows of arches, as the architrave had virtually died out. The sole function

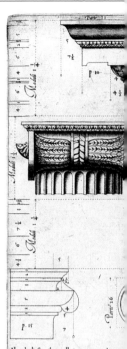

Il modo di fare il capitello Ionico ancora che nella presente carta sia designato con la pianta et profilo a piu chiara intelligentia si deue trar due linee a perpendicolo duoi moduli lontano una dall'altra le quali passano per il centro de gli occhi delle uolute et sono chiamate Catheti. Tutta la uoluta deue essere alta 16 parti di modulo 8 restano sopra l'occhio il quale è duoe parti et le sei restano di sotto. Il modo col quale si fanno queste uolute è disegnato nella seguente carta et in sara anco breuemente scritto per quanto comporta lo spatio il modo con che si procede.

x VIII

Vignola described the orders in detail in his manual of 1562 (above); the plates illustrate each order in plan and in profile.

of the round pillars in church naves and the small columns in triforia (upper galleries) or cloisters was to support rows of arches.

The return of the column

One of the first achievements of Brunelleschi, the father of the Renaissance in architecture, was the revival of classical systems of support. On the façade of the Ospedale degli Innocenti in Florence he designed in 1421 a portico with columns, although continuing the medieval practice of using them to support arches. Yet he framed the portico with heavy, grooved pilasters on either side and these supported a continuous entablature. The distinctively classical features had been returned to prominence. Inside the sacristy of San Lorenzo and in the Pazzi Chapel he used an entablature above pilasters. In the naves of both Santo Spirito and San Lorenzo he managed to reconcile classical and medieval practice by placing a section of entablature between the arches and columns of the nave; in the aisles of San Lorenzo, however, he followed the classical model exactly, with a continuous entablature supported by pilasters, which touches the tops of the arches of the side chapels opening off the aisle. The vocabulary of antiquity was re-established forthwith. The segment of entablature invented by Brunelleschi was to remain the usual way of joining arches to columns. The return to the use of the entablature was one of the defining characteristics of the

The Ospedale degli Innocenti in Florence (opposite below), the first non-ecclesiastical building by Brunelleschi (above), uses columns, round arches, medallions in the spandrels, a classical entablature and windows above the arches. In Santo Spirito Brunelleschi perfected the structure of his columns by placing a segment of entablature between the capital and the arch (below).

Renaissance style; the decorative scalloped effect created by a row of arches was made more sober and disciplined by the geometrical effect of continuous horizontal lines.

The orders

Brunelleschi and his successors could not fail to have noticed that the proportions of columns varied according the their 'ornaments' (to use Vitruvius' term), that is the types of capital and entablature allocated to them. By studying archaeological remains and by reading Vitruvius they were able to work out the theory governing the different types, and to revive it. The different types of capital were named after the style of ornament that had defined them in antiquity, but because each type was the material expression of a whole system of proportion they were given the general name of orders.

The system was based on an elementary optical illusion: if a building has several storeys of equal height, the upper storeys seem to lose height the higher they are, because of their distance from a spectator standing at ground level. The building appears to shrink as it rises. All that was needed to correct this optical illusion was to make the storeys progressively higher. The orders were used to establish the

In one of the plates drawn to complete the illustrations taken from Fra Giocondo in the first French edition of Vitruvius' treatise (1547), Jean Goujon, an architect as well as a sculptor, shows the architect standing at ground level observing the proportions of the upper parts of a classical-style building: the entablature, the pediment and a statue on a raised pedestal.

to il Catheto di questa prima uoluta et un'altra linea in sguadro che passi per il
tro dell' occhio si diuide il detto occhio nel modo segnato di sopra nella figura
et si comincia poi al primo punto segnato 1 et si gira col compasso una quar-
'i circolo dipoi al punto segnato 2 si gira l'altra quarta et cosi procedendo si

The Ionic order is characterized by its volute capital seen in profile, framed by a band of egg-and-dart. The design of the volute exercised Renaissance architects considerably, and they sought a geometrical method of procuring the perfect shape. In 1552 the Venetian painter Giuseppe Porta, known as Salviati, published a 'Rule for drawing the volute of the Ionic capital with dividers', and his method was endorsed by the architect of the Mantuan court, Giovanni Battista Bertani, in his 'Obscure and difficult passages from Vitruvius on the Ionic order' (1558). This plate from Vignola's manual (left) publicized the method. In contrast to the virile Doric order, the Ionic was considered to have been inspired by the proportions of the female body and it was given a female character.

correct relationship between the different heights. Each order had its own proportions. In other words, its height was fixed in relation to the width of the column. A different order, higher than the one below, was therefore allocated to each storey of a building. In this way the elevation was prevented from looking squashed; indeed the effect was to make it look as if it opened out as it got closer to the top. A building like the Colosseum provides a demonstration of this theory.

Greek architecture used three basic orders: Doric, Ionic and Corinthian. The Romans added two variants, Tuscan and Composite. The first builders of Renaissance Italy in the 15th century had difficulty recognizing the different types, particularly because the only surviving classical treatise was by an architect of the Augustan period, Vitruvius, and most of the surviving monuments dated from much later – from the end of the Roman Empire for the most part – and did not conform to his prescriptions. The discrepancies between visible reality and out-of-date theory had to be resolved. A logical and straightforward new theory took shape. Finally, in 1562, Vignola published a definitive codification of the orders in his *Regola delle cinque ordini.*

In this juxtaposition of all the orders on a single plate, Vignola shows their distinctive features and different proportions.

The five classical orders

The Doric order is of stocky proportions and looks the sturdiest. It can be identified by its capital, which is moulded but bears no other ornamentation, and by the type of entablature surmounting it: a plain architrave, then a layer of straight panels with triple fluting reminiscent of the beams placed over the architrave in wooden buildings. Triglyphs (panels with three grooves) and metopes (sculpted panels) alternate and are decorated with relief motifs (ox skulls, paterae – discs). The cornice above is supported by simple cuboid consoles. The Tuscan order, a variant of the Doric, is stockier and even plainer, easily distinguishable by the absence of triglyphs and metopes. The Ionic order is more slender. Its capitals have symmetrical volutes, seen from the front, and a more highly decorated entablature with a carved frieze above the architrave. The Corinthian order is more elongated, and its capitals covered in acanthus decorated with scrolls at the diagonals and a rosette in the middle. The entablature bears more rows of decoration than the Ionic. The Composite order is built to the same proportions as the Corinthian but differs in its decoration: its capitals combine the Corinthian

TOSCANO   DORICO   IONICO

acanthus with the Ionic volutes, which are placed on the diagonals.

The relationship between the orders

According to the canon established by Vignola, the five orders are linked by their proportion, their height being calculated from the same module, the diameter of the column: the Tuscan order is 7 modules high, the Doric 8, the Ionic 9 and the Corinthian and the Composite 10. In general, because of its simplicity, the Tuscan order was reserved for more rustic purposes – country villas, for instance, or defensive buildings like city gates and fortresses. The Doric order, the most robust and virile of those in general use, was devoted to the ground floor, which bears the weight of the whole building. The Ionic was used for the first floor, and the Corinthian or Composite for the second. This sequence was not established, however, until later.

When Alberti reintroduced the

The authors of the various treatises all had their own version of the classical orders. In *Architecture* (1567) Philibert Delorme gives a detailed account of the Corinthian capital and entablature that he used in the chapel of the château at Villers-Cotterêts (1552, above). The normal module for any order was the diameter of the column. G. B. Montano demonstrated it visually (left) by drawing the number of circumferences required inside the shaft of the column.

CORINTHO   COMPOSITO

superposition of orders on the façade of the Palazzo Rucellai in the mid-15th century, he was using them fairly randomly. The earliest and most obvious faithful imitation of a classical model was the courtyard of the Palazzo Venezia in Rome, which was built in about

At the Vatican Bramante was responsible for the left wing of the courtyard of San Damasio (left), where he applied the classical orders: three arcaded storeys with Doric, Ionic and Corinthian pilasters.

1470. Bramante built the first example of the correct superposition of the three orders at the Vatican in 1514; this established the hierarchy, and made the use of orders almost obligatory. Some of the noblest edifices of the century were the result – the interior courtyard of the Palazzo Farnese in Rome, Palladio's cloister in the Carità in Venice and the Procuratie Nuove in St Mark's Square.

The choice of order

There were always divergences from the rules, and eccentric solutions were also possible. It was quite acceptable to use an order other than the Doric on the ground floor provided there were no lesser orders above it. Even in 1559 Sanmicheli surmounted the Corinthian columns of the Palazzo Grimani on the Grand Canal in Venice with another set of Corinthian columns on the first floor. In 1568 Francesco Primaticcio put the Tuscan order on the first floor of his new wing at Fontainebleau. In general, however, if a single order was used in a building, for example inside a church, it was usually Corinthian that was chosen for its elegant ornament, and Corinthian therefore became the most widespread.

At the beginning of the 16th century Bramante designed a new type of façade in which only the *piano nobile*, the first floor, had columns on it; the masonry of the ground floor was dressed to look rough and rustic. This practice became very popular all over Italy and was used by Sanmicheli in Verona and by Palladio on the Palazzo Thiene in Vicenza.

The giant order

A single row of columns or pilasters can be used through two storeys of a building to produce a more imposing effect, and this technique is known as the giant order; columns of colossal scale can in fact belong to any order. Brunelleschi gave an example in the unfinished Palazzo di Parte Guelfa in Florence. The idea was revived in the 16th century with some very ambitious façades. The giant order could begin at first-floor level, as in Sanmicheli's *palazzi* in Verona, or in the

After the death of Bramante in 1514, his successor Raphael completed this wing with a loggia and open colonnade under the entablature. In this 19th-century painting Horace Vernet depicted Raphael in the corner of his courtyard (opposite right).

In the new wing he designed for the château at Fontainebleau in 1568 (below), Primaticcio used a Corinthian church façade design by Serlio for the centre and an order of Tuscan pilasters on the first storey. This very unusual solution aroused no adverse criticism and the Tuscan order was extended to all the façades on the courtyard, including Ange-Jacques Gabriel's Grand Pavilion erected in 1751.

Palazzo dei Senatori in Rome, but more usual were giant columns starting at ground level. The order was used in this manner during the 16th century by Giulio Romano in the Palazzo del Tè in Mantua, by Michelangelo in the Palazzo dei Conservatori on the Capitoline and by Palladio in the Palazzo Valmarana and the Loggia del Capitaniato in Vicenza.

One of the essential features of classical architecture was the portico or pronaos with colossal columns supporting a pediment attached to the façade of the building. Alberti used this design for the façade of the church of Sant'Andrea in Mantua in the last thirty years of the 15th century, but he made do with pilasters. The true portico was more or less incompatible with contemporary building design, and it would have fallen into disuse if Palladio had not revived it in the second half of the 16th century. He used it as the distinctive feature of the façades of his villas, including (amongst others) the Villa Foscara (La Malcontenta) at Mira (1560) and Villa Capra, better known as the Villa Rotunda, just outside Vicenza (begun c. 1567–9); if circumstances did not permit free-standing columns he would attach them to the wall, as he did at the Villa Barbaro at Maser and on the façades of the churches he designed for Venice – San Giorgio Maggiore (completed by Vincenzo Scamozzi), San Francesco della Vigna and the Redentore. Just before his death in 1580, however, he reaffirmed his preference for the pronaos, using it on the façade of the chapel or *tempietto* at Maser.

In the Old Sacristy in San Lorenzo, Brunelleschi used an order of pilasters that was an early version of the 'giant' order, embracing two storeys (the door and the bas-relief over it, above). By framing the door with much smaller Ionic columns he was juxtaposing a 'major' and a 'minor' order in a way that was later to become common.

The spread of the orders

In the 16th century the orders spread beyond the confines of Italy. In France their use remained empirical throughout the reign of François I. The first examples of the correct superposition of orders was the gate (now gone) at Ecouen, c. 1545, probably by Jean Goujon, and the central 'frontispiece' at Anet (re-erected after the Revolution in the courtyard of the Ecole des Beaux-Arts in Paris), designed by Philibert Delorme shortly before 1550. In his *Reigle générale d'architecture* (1564), Jean Bullant published the first practical manual in French, but this failed to outshine Vignola's work.

The progress of the orders was somewhat slower in Spain, in spite of the fact that Diego de Sagredo, in 1526, had discussed them in his adaptation of Vitruvius entitled 'The Proportions of Roman architecture' (*Medidas del Romano*) of 1526. The use of orders at the Irish College in Salamanca around 1530 was still empirical; the design for the façade of the Hospital de la Sagrada Sangre in Seville in the 1560s was somewhat more accurate, but

The giant order was generally confined to the façades of monumental buildings, as here at Sant' Andrea in Mantua (above). Alberti used colossal Corinthian columns on the triumphal arch (designed in 1472) that acts as a façade. Giulio Romano used it on all the external walls of the Palazzo del Tè, also in Mantua, erected in 1525 (below). This low and strongly horizontal building owes its monumental appearance to the use of the giant order (opposite).

To match the projecting bay that he was designing for the north wing, and to provide a suitably monumental setting for Michelangelo's *Slaves*, which the *connétable* of Montmorency had just bought, Jean Bullant added this portico (left) with colossal Corinthian columns to the south wing of the château of Ecouen (built in 1539 in a very simple style). It overwhelms the original elevation completely. Michelangelo's statues were transferred to the Louvre long ago, but plaster casts have recently been installed in the two niches, to complete the composition.

the proportions were still reversed. Shortly afterwards, however, the Escorial was built with orders superimposed correctly. The orders spread to northern Europe even more gradually, except when Italian architects like Pasqualini at Juliers or Friedrich Sustris, the Italianized Fleming, at Landshut and Munich, were involved. Although Rivius published a manual of the five orders in Germany in 1547, the handling of the orders in the Ott-Heinrichsbau in Heidelberg (about 1560) is still very clumsy, and there is no known 16th-century example of the correct superposition of the three orders in the German Empire.

Outside Italy the giant order seems to have been widely used only in France. Bullant, with his taste for the grandiose, used it at Chantilly (in the Petit Château), at Fère-en-Tardenois and in the courtyard at Ecouen; it became fashionable under the last of the Valois kings (ruling until 1589), when large-scale projects were popular. It can be found in all the large

buildings of the day (Charleval, Verneuil, St Maur) recorded by Androuet du Cerceau, and in the western part of the Grande Galerie of the Louvre, built under Henry IV. The Hôtel de Diane d'Angoulême (now the Bibliothèque Historique de la Ville de Paris) is one of the few surviving examples of this fashion. Spain, however, did not entirely ignore the giant order, at least in ecclesiastical architecture; it can be found in the interior of the cathedral in Granada and in the cathedral in Jaén.

A choice

The Renaissance predilection for the classical orders was just that; it should not be thought of as a restrictive rule. The use of columns and pilasters was never obligatory. Beauty could only be achieved if the general principles of regularity, symmetry, geometry and proportion were observed. Many important Renaissance buildings, some of them even stylistically significant, bore no columns on their façade at all. This was generally the case with the Florentine *palazzo* (Medici, Pitti, Strozzi) as it developed during the 15th century. Thanks to Antonio da Sangallo the Florentine influence reached Rome in the 16th century and can be detected on great palaces, including the Palazzo Farnese. The Lonja in Saragossa, Lescot's façades at the Louvre and the castle of Aschaffenburg are further examples.

Antonio da Sangallo the Younger designed the façade of the Palazzo Farnese in Rome (below, and the entrance above) in the Florentine manner, with orders only in the interior courtyard. He used small columns to frame the windows and rusticated quoins on the corners. The top storey is by Michelangelo.

The dome

The orders were not the only important new features of Renaissance architectural language. Other elements such as vaulting, ornament and mouldings also need to be considered. Of the first, the innovative items were the dome and vault, both on pendentives, which are concave triangles looking as if they had been cut from a sphere. The dome had been used by the Romans and also during the Romanesque period, at that time

The earliest domes of the Renaissance, like Brunelleschi's in the Old Sacristy of San Lorenzo (left), were circular pointed vaults, built like an umbrella directly on to the pendentives, without a drum. As a result they were shallow and dark, in spite of the openings at the base of the spokes of the vault. The dome of Florence Cathedral (centre), conceived in the 14th century, rests on a deep octagonal drum and its curved shape is still Gothic.

usually being supported on squinches, that is on half-cone-shaped brackets placed in the corners; it had practically disappeared from Gothic architecture. The Renaissance brought the dome back, supporting it now on pendentives. The pendentive ensures a successful transition from the square plan over the crossing of a church (the usual shape) to the circular dome and its drum, offering scope for decoration at the same time. The normal practice in Italy was to place painted medallions, generally depicting the Evangelists, in the pendentives. Brunelleschi's construction of the enormous dome on Florence Cathedral has encouraged many people to consider this as the starting point of the Renaissance in architecture. This is a misconception, however, since the project dates back to the 14th century. Brunelleschi's achievement was to have built it without either scaffolding or timber centring to support it; it was more a feat of engineering than of architecture.

Nevertheless, its success undoubtedly contributed to the spread of the dome, which became one of the basic features of Renaissance architecture.

The drum and the dome

Apart from the dome of Florence Cathedral (whose drum is also unusual), the earliest domes were built directly on top of the pendentives, and it was common practice to disguise them from the outside with a vertical masonry *tiburio* or drum. This can be seen in Santa Maria della Carceri in Prato, in all the 15th-century domed churches in Lombardy, and, in a later version, in Santa Maria della Passione in Milan. This way of building had the disadvantage of depriving the crossing of natural light.

In the 15th century the centrally planned church began to be recognized as the most perfect architectural structure. The usual shape was based on a Greek cross, with a dome over the crossing. In the 16th century the drum was added, which raised the height of the dome and illuminated the crossing. The church of the Madonna di San Biagio at Montepulciano, begun in 1518 to designs by Antonio da Sangallo the Elder, is one of the handsomest examples (above). Only the apse at the east end and the two bell towers beside the façade indicate the direction in which the church faces.

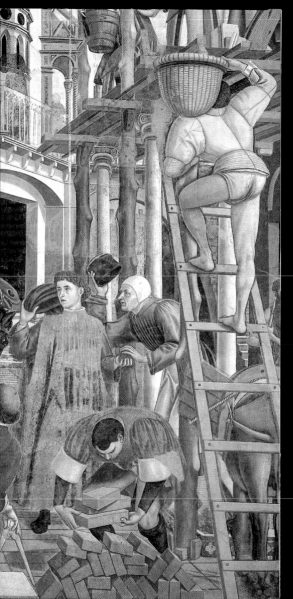

A building site in the 15th century

In a fresco painted for the Ospedale di Santa Maria della Scala in Siena (1443), Domenico di Bartolo shows a bishop distributing alms in a piazza where builders are working. The man with dividers in the front seems to be taking measurements from a plan, another is picking up bricks, a third climbing a ladder with a hod on his shoulder. A bucket of cement has been carried by pulley up on to the scaffolding. In spite of such realistic touches, the buildings, structurally quite incoherent and exuberantly decorated, are unrealistic and arbitrary, typical of Sienese painting.

A building site in the early 16th century

On the left a cart with large blocks o stone is being unloaded and two masons are beginning to shape them. In the middle a cornice is being cut and a large beam transported. On the right (detail left) the architect is overseeing the carving of the shaft of a column. In the background a building in the classical style is being erected.

It also concealed the presence of the dome from outside. It was only at the beginning of the 16th century that a cylindrical drum began to be placed between the pendentives and the dome, with windows that allowed light to fall on the crossing. At the same time the old practice (kept alive in St Mark's in Venice and in the Basilica del Santo in Padua) of displaying the shape of the interior dome on the outside by covering it with a wooden dome was revived.

Bramante's *tempietto* at San Pietro in Montorio, the Madonna di San Biagio at Montepulciano and Santa Maria della Consolazione at Todi all demonstrate the superiority of the drum, which made the interior brighter and the exterior more impressive. It began to be universally adopted – by Galeazzo Alessi in Santa Maria di Carignano in Genoa, by Sanmicheli in the church of the Madonna di Campagna in Verona, by Palladio in San Giorgio

The function of the lantern is to cover the hole at the top of a dome and to admit as much light as possible. Brunelleschi provided a model for the lantern over the dome of Florence Cathedral (above) just before his death (1446), thereby establishing the shape of the small *tempietto* that was to remain standard.

Maggiore in Venice and by Michelangelo in St Peter's in Rome. Following the example set in the Florence Cathedral it became common practice to open the dome at the top and to cover the opening with a lantern in the shape of a *tempietto*, a finishing touch in the classical manner.

The pendentive vault

Brunelleschi introduced another type of ceiling in the portico of the Ospedale degli Innocenti and

in the aisles of the churches he designed; this was the pendentive vault, which consists of four pendentives joined together to form a dome shape resting on a point at each corner. This type of structure, built without the traditional groins or ribs, permits the construction of a smooth vault whose regular curve echoes the curve of the rounded arches used from this time on. It remained a speciality of Florentine architecture, but other examples can be found in Italy and Spain, for example in the cathedral in Jaén.

The side-aisles in the church of San Lorenzo in Florence bear all the features of Brunelleschi's new vocabulary: the pilasters separating the individual chapels match the columns of the arcade; the vaults on pendentives between the pairs of arches echo the curve of all the round arches. The same language could be applied perfectly well to non-ecclesiastical architecture: the structure of this aisle and the elevation of nave is virtually the same as in the Ospedale degli Innocenti, where a portico with columns and vaults in pendentives is surmounted by a façade with large rectangular windows.

The circular building with a dome was the ideal. Opposite bottom: a commemorative chapel in Rome designed by Bramante to mark the spot where St Peter was martyred; it retained the (not particularly appropriate) name of *tempietto*, little temple.

Giovanni Antonio Amadeo introduced the Florentine style into Lombardy with his centrally planned funerary chapel built for the Condottiere Bartolomeo Colleoni next to Santa Maria Maggiore in Bergamo (1470). Amadeo's training as a sculptor, combined with local tradition, inspired a style of exterior decoration that obliterates the geometrical simplicity of the structure: inlaid marble, plus a riot of sculpture and statuary on plinths and pinnacles, like a final flowering of the Gothic style that was so frowned upon by partisans of the Renaissance.

Ornament

Classical decoration was also given a new lease of life. Gothic architecture had used only simple crockets to start with, followed later by bands of deeply carved foliage, with a kind of curly-headed cabbage on the pinnacles. The Renaissance stamped out such frivolities and re-established stylized classical ornament, using purely geometrical motifs like the Greek key pattern, bars, strings of beads, the egg-and-dart pattern, grooves or naturalistic motifs treated geometrically: foliage, interlacing or in bands, or candelabra patterns rising vertically to support a vase. Gothic designs were only gradually replaced by classical forms. In Lombardy and the Veneto capitals were very imaginatively decorated with naturalistic motifs until the early 16th century; there were dolphins in the friezes and the branching

foliage on the pilasters was dotted with birds and insects, and other whimsical additions. The Colleoni Chapel in Bergamo and Santa Maria de' Miracoli in Venice typify this style of decoration; it was very popular in France until the 1530s and in Spain for the first half of the century, but in both countries it gave way (as it did in Italy) to classical ornament. The simplest type of decoration, moulding, which provides a frame or draws the spectator's eye to different levels, was also revived along classical lines. In the Middle Ages mouldings were carved on to the existing wall. In the Renaissance relief moulding was carved in advance and built in. Entablatures and window and door frames stood out from the wall, like picture frames, catching the light and enhancing the architecture with their shadows.

Rustication

The very masonry itself underwent a transformation. Rustication, reserved for military architecture during the Middle Ages, was introduced into civil buildings,

In the 15th century rustication became the characteristic feature of the façades of Florentine palaces, and remained so in spite of the popularity of the classical orders. The Palazzo Strozzi (begun 1489, below) was decorated with rustication. Among a number of varieties, the pointed diamond cut was in vogue for a while in the second half of the century, but disappeared later. It can be found in Naples, Bologna and in Ferrara on the *palazzo* built by Biagio Rossetti for Sigismondo d'Este in about 1492, the Palazzo dei Diamanti (below left). It was even introduced by an Italian to Moscow.

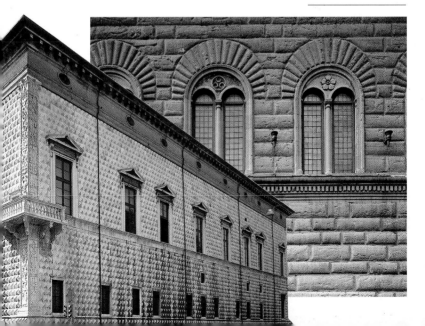

probably through the influence of the Florentine *palazzo,* which was traditionally a fortified building. It spread rapidly and produced some picturesque effects, soon becoming the usual style of masonry for the ground floor of palaces, and being used even more widely to accentuate corners or to frame bays. There were all sorts of variants. The Florentine style consisted of stone blocks deliberately left to look as though they had come straight from the quarry; it developed into blocks with a rough or sponge-like surface, or smooth with recessed joints (as in the façade of San Michele in Venice), or with diamond-shaped points (Palazzo dei Diamanti in Ferrara). France adopted rustication readily and added to the repertory of shapes, with banded rustication, chamfered to create horizontal channels, or vermiculated rustication (resembling worm-casts), very popular at the end of the century, used for example on the Grande Galerie of the Louvre.

Artistic licence

One unforeseen consequence of introducing the strict rules of the new architectural language was that any infringement of the rules, or any anomaly, caused surprise or even shock. Such a reaction would not have occurred before the new norms had been established. Yet freedom of expression in the Middle Ages was, in fact, illusory, as it is only in cases where there are rules that they can they be broken. Giulio Romano was the first architect to introduce deliberate anomalies with the aim of surprising and entertaining: column shafts and keystones left unexpectedly rough-hewn. Michelangelo would redesign forms and ornament to suit his own purposes: the high windows in the New Sacristy of San Lorenzo in Florence are trapezoid to give an effect of perspective. Or he would use the rules in a contradictory way, tucking the columns in the vestibule of the Biblioteca Laurenziana in Florence into the walls. Only those familiar with the rules realized that liberties were being taken. Paradoxically, the doctrine now established had given to innovative spirits new scope for originality.

Three different ways of bending the rules. In the Palacio de Miranda in Burgos (1545, above) the architect designed capitals modelled on wooden consoles. In the courtyard of the Palazzo del Tè in Mantua (1526, right) Giulio Romano designed parts of the entablature to look as if they were slipping out of position. In the entrance to the Biblioteca Laurenziana in Florence (far right) Michelangelo recessed columns into the walls.

Renaissance building programmes were similar to those in the Middle Ages, and consisted mainly of the construction of churches and palaces or, north of the Alps, châteaux. Italy added two new types of building only: the country house or villa and the uniformly planned public square.

CHAPTER 4

NEW BUILDING TYPES

Pope Leo X inspects a model of the façade of the church of San Lorenzo (the parish church of the Medici), presented to him by Michelangelo. On the table there is a plan of the Biblioteca Laurenziana. Right: the Villa Medici at Poggio a Caiano.

The lessons of Brunelleschi

As soon as Brunelleschi began producing his innovative designs in Florence, religious architecture underwent a fundamental change. In San Lorenzo and Santo Spirito he used the traditional Latin-cross plan, but combined it with the classical basilica, returning to the principle of a roofed nave bordered by columns, and adding a dome over the crossing. In the sacristy of San Lorenzo (also a Medici funerary chapel) he adopted a square plan covered by a dome, producing a variant of this in the Pazzi Chapel in Santa Croce. His design for Santa Maria degli Angeli (unfortunately never finished) was a rotunda with chapels radiating from it. In smaller buildings he used the centralized plan (that is, a single space that could be enclosed within a circle), which had

Brunelleschi presents the model of the church of San Lorenzo to Cosimo I de' Medici; from a fresco by Vasari in the Palazzo Vecchio in Florence (above, and detail right). In order to compete for work, and to impress the patrons, princes and prelates, architects made extremely detailed models of their designs.

virtually disappeared since the days of the Romanesque baptistry. His work had a considerable influence. The basilica form used by Brunelleschi in his larger churches was re-used, with variations, in the 15th century by Giuliano da Sangallo (perhaps) in the cathedral of Cortona, by Giuliano da Maiano in that of Faenza, by Biagio Rossetti in the churches of San Francesco and Santa Maria in Vado in Ferrara and by Mauro Codussi in San Michele in Venice. In the 16th century Giulio Romano's plan for Mantua Cathedral was also influenced by Brunelleschi.

Of the various designs prepared by Michelangelo in 1559 for the church of San Giovanni dei Fiorentini in Rome, the one approved by Pope Julius III was particularly

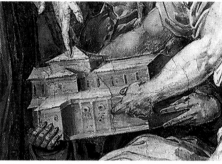

The centralized plan

The centralized plan was immensely successful and became the standard plan for the votive churches being built all over Italy to glorify miraculous images of the Virgin. Giuliano da Sangallo designed the perfect example of a church based on a Greek cross in the Santa Maria delle Carceri in Prato.

innovative (below left). Instead of the usual type of Greek-cross shape, contained in a square, where the chapels fill in the corners, he designed a star-shaped church with chapels opening into the central space. The dome was to be supported on eight columns in a circle, not the traditional four columns in the diagonals. The crossing was a perfectly symmetrical rotunda. Instead of the usual right angles, the exterior was to have curved walls, which Michelangelo also used for St Peter's.

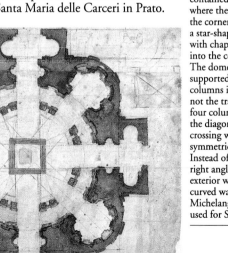

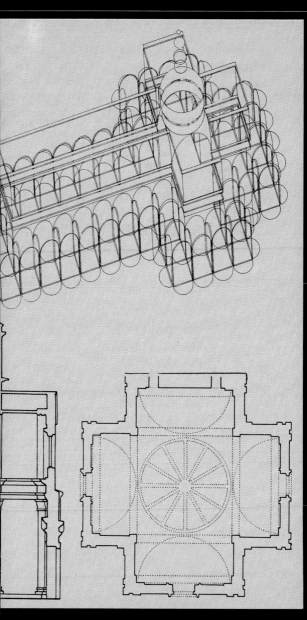

Brunelleschi's original plan for the church of Santo Spirito (opposite top and left) had chapels all round, even on the façade; these would have caused curious undulations around the outside elevation. The builders, however, did not keep to his plan. The chapels on the façade were not compatible with the usual three entrances and were eliminated. A straight wall hid the curved ends of the others. The plan was based on a square module (the crossing measuring four times the area of one of the aisle bays). Santa Maria delle Carceri in Prato (below left) by Giuliano da Sangallo follows the strict Greek-cross plan with no corner chapels. The four equal arms are roofed with a barrel vault and the crossing with a dome on pendentives (bottom opposite and centre). The dome is still 'umbrella-shaped', but invisible from outside; the vestigial drum is very low. Light comes through small holes at the lower edge of the vaults of the dome. Giuliano da Sangallo proved himself the heir to Brunelleschi. This church is the summary of developments made during the 15th century, rather than the harbinger of things to come.

The sacristy of Santo Spirito in Florence is of an octagonal type. At the end of the century Lombard architects proposed various seductive variations on the theme: a square plan with an octagonal dome at Santa Maria de Canepanova in Pavia and, at Busto Arsizio, an octagonal plan for the Incoronata in Lodi, a rotunda with four equal arms in Crema, a Greek cross with an octagonal crossing in Santa Maria della Passione in Milan. In Venice Mauro Codussi seized the opportunity to reintroduce the Byzantine quincunx plan in San Giovanni Grisostomo. Somewhat behind Florence in the 15th century, Rome also discovered the centralized structure with the founding of the church of Santa Maria della Pace by Sixtus IV. In the 16th century the form was used by almost all the great architects: Bramante in San Pietro in Montorio in Rome (rotunda), then in the first plan for St Peter's and (if he is its author, as seems probable) at Santa Maria della Consolazione at Todi (a quatrefoil); Michelangelo in the New Sacristy for San Lorenzo in Florence (a classical square) and particularly in his plan for St Peter's, Rome (another Greek cross); Galeazzo Alessi in Santa Maria di Carignano in Genoa (a quincunx); Sanmicheli in the Madonna di Campagna in Verona (an octagon in a rotunda); and Palladio in the chapel at Maser (a circle).

Mixed types of building

The centralized structure was ill-suited to accommodate large crowds and in very busy churches the longitudinal plan remained a necessity. In the 15th century the idea arose of mixing the two types by building a sanctuary with a centralized plan at the end of the nave: this compromise solution was used by Michelozzo for the SS. Annunziata in Florence, by Alberti for the Tempio Malatestiano in Rimini, by Piero Lombardo for San Giobbe and Santa Maria de' Miracoli in Venice and by Bramante in Santa Maria delle Grazie in Milan. Pavia Cathedral could also be considered to have adopted the same plan: the dome covers the crossing plus the aisles, and the crossing is therefore broader than the nave, which makes it a structure in its own right, rather than a straightforward transept crossing.

Bramante's first plan for the reconstruction of St Peter's in Rome, on a Greek-cross plan, is known only from this half plan (above).

The combination of the Latin-cross shape with a dome was a constant aim during the Renaissance. Matteo de' Pasti's medal (below) is the only surviving reference to Alberti's plan for the Tempio Malatestiano in Rimini, which he was unable to complete. At one end of the original nave, concealed beneath a classical 'skin', he planned a vast dome over the sanctuary that would have dominated the entire composition. Pavia Cathedral, the plan of which (left) has been drawn from the large wooden model, shows a crossing developed to such an extent that it looks like a Greek cross to which a short nave (of five bays) has been added.

This combination might be justified by the additional funerary role of the sanctuary, as in the SS. Annunziata in Florence, in the Tempio Malatestiano in Rimini, in Santa Maria delle Grazie in Milan or, in the 16th century, Granada Cathedral, but it was not very successful. The traditional Latin cross still prevailed; the influence of the centralized plan was simply to add a dome over the crossing, following Brunelleschi's example. Alberti adopted this solution for Sant'Andrea in Mantua and Francesco di Giorgio for the Santa Maria di Calcinaio near Cortona; finally, Bramante used it for the design of the new St Peter's, begun in 1506, and indeed it became far

the most commonly used layout for churches in the 16th century.

The Council of Trent (1545–63) advocated that churches should lend themselves easily to the celebration of the Mass in the presence of a large congregation; in design terms, this implied a broad nave with no side-aisles. The type described above was therefore simplified to achieve the design perfected by Vignola in the Gesù in Rome, and universally copied: a nave bordered by chapels and a sanctuary planned like a

centralized structure, covered by a dome and prolonged eastwards by an apse. The altar was always placed in the apse and the transepts were reduced to two side-chapels broadened to accommodate the dimensions of the dome. There was no crossing as such and the dome, having become obligatory in churches aspiring to beauty, was simply there for aesthetic reasons. This type of structure was predominant in the last third of the 16th century, with variations. In the Redentore in Venice, Palladio gave the sanctuary a trefoil shape.

The church façade

The Renaissance changed the façade to make it compatible with its own principles of composition and design.

In Sant' Andrea in Mantua (opposite, 1472), Alberti provided an early example of a church with a single, very broad nave, ending in a crossing covered by a dome (the present one was erected in the 18th century, but the arrangement of the piers proves that it was part of the original plan). The Gesù in Rome (left) conforms to the recommendations that followed the Council of Trent; it is designed as a Latin cross with a single nave but the crossing with its dome constitutes the main space of the church. Andrea Sacchi's painting, showing the interior before the addition of the Baroque decoration, gives an idea of the simple, dignified architecture of Vignola.

In spite of the vision of Bramante and Michelangelo, St Peter's in Rome was finally given a nave; the huge area under the dome nevertheless serves as a reminder of the fascination for Renaissance architects of the centralized plan. This early 17th-century anonymous painting gives valuable information about the appearance of the basilica before the Baroque decoration was added. The vault over the nave had already been gilded (in 1616) but the apse was still 'the colour of travertine', as Michelangelo wished.

It was Alberti who introduced the orders and, at the end of his life, he also tried (in Sant' Andrea in Mantua) to treat the façade like a triumphal arch by using the giant order. At Santa Maria Novella in Florence he designed two storeys of orders, one on top of the other, the lower order corresponding to the whole width of the building, the upper one to the nave only. The upper order forms a kind of frontispiece or pediment to the other part and is joined to the side-aisles by volutes. This design became the most popular and the most widely used of all. Variations did occur – in the width of the upper storey, the shape and number of supports (usually a mixture of columns and pilasters) and in the design of the pediment, but the overall layout was generally preserved. The only other design was initiated by Palladio and consisted of a giant portico in front of the nave, with the volutes replaced by the angles of another imagined pediment that is almost hidden by this portico. The result looks like a conflict between two structures with very different façades, a broad and low one that is almost completely hidden behind the other much larger one; horizontal divisions disappear, the vertical nave reasserts itself, and the internal structure is expressed on the outside.

In Santa Maria Novella in Florence (centre) Alberti created the model of the new church façade. The central upper part is joined to the lower aisles by huge volutes. At the chapel or *tempietto* next to the Villa Barbaro at Maser (left, 1580) Palladio echoed the design of the Pantheon, placing a classical portico (pronaos) with giant columns in front of the rotunda.

The church outside Italy

In other countries the time was not yet ripe for Italian church design to be adopted completely. In France the Gothic tradition was too strong to be swept aside suddenly: Gothic architecture continued to set the style, although Renaissance detail began to creep in, as can be seen in the church of St-Eustache in Paris. The centralized structure was only permitted in special cases, for example in privately financed chapels in cathedrals or in châteaux. Philibert Delorme built chapels like those at St-Germain-en-Laye (a trefoil plan with a pronaos), at St-Léger and at Anet – the latter being the only surviving one.

In the German-speaking countries the endurance of Gothic architecture, reinforced by the extraordinary flowering of the Flamboyant style, was even stronger. It was not until Friedrich Sustris intervened with his design for the Jesuit church in Munich, that Vignola's models were adapted, and even then the church was without a dome.

The chapels designed by Philibert Delorme were all centrally planned, with a dome. The chapel at Anet (below) is a Greek cross in a square, but has some unusual features: the arms are curved at the ends; doors open within the corner piers; the dome is decorated with coffering in perspective, whose design is repeated in the paving.

Spain was more receptive to Italian models.
The centralized plan was applied in various ways:
the chapel devoted to relics in the cathedral of
Sigüenza was square, the sacristy of Seville Cathedral
twelve-sided, the church in the Escorial shaped like
a Greek cross. In Granada Cathedral and the church
in Ubeda the Latin-cross shape was combined with
an imposing circular sanctuary. In the Hospital
de la Sagrada Sangre in Seville and in St John
the Baptist in Toledo there was a dome over
the crossing.

The Italian palace

The most important type of civil building in Italy was
the *palazzo*, the large urban dwelling of the aristocracy
or rich bourgeoisie who typically lived in towns, whereas
north of the Alps the nobility lived in châteaux on
their own estates. Traditionally, the Italian palace was
a block built round a central courtyard, to a square
or quadrangular plan and looking very massive from
the outside, but with plenty of loggias and balconies
opening on to the courtyard. The general style remained
unchanged, but the plan was made considerably more
regular and the outside elevations altered markedly by

In the mid-15th
century, the
Palazzo Medici (left)
established the style of
the Florentine *palazzo*:
square courtyard with
arcades around the four
sides. In Rome, Antonio
da Sangallo the Younger
used the style in the
antique manner for his
Palazzo Farnese (above);
the arcades rest, not on
simple columns, but
on piers, which bear
the engaged columns
of the first order.

the introduction of orders. Florentine *palazzi* retained their austere exteriors, making extensive use of rusticated stone; Alberti's Palazzo Rucellai with its rows of pilasters on the outside was imitated only in the Palazzo Piccolomini in Pienza. On the inside, however, although the arcades on the ground floor of the courtyard continued to be supported by columns throughout the 15th century, the upper storeys soon came in for the classical treatment. The first floor of the courtyard of the palace in Urbino is given pilasters, and the top floor of the Medici and Strozzi palaces in Florence have loggias with architraves.

The most exact reproductions of the Roman style could be found in Rome, first in the courtyard of the so-called Palazzo Venezia, which for years was the sole example, then in Bramante's designs for the courtyard of San Damasio at the Vatican.

B ramante designed a new type of façade for the Palazzo Caprini in Rome (1501, below): the rusticated ground floor housed shops in the classical manner. The first floor, the *piano nobile*, bore an order of paired Doric columns. Raphael used the same type of front elevation for his Palazzo Vidoni-Caffarelli, and Palladio was influenced by it in his *palazzi* in Vicenza.

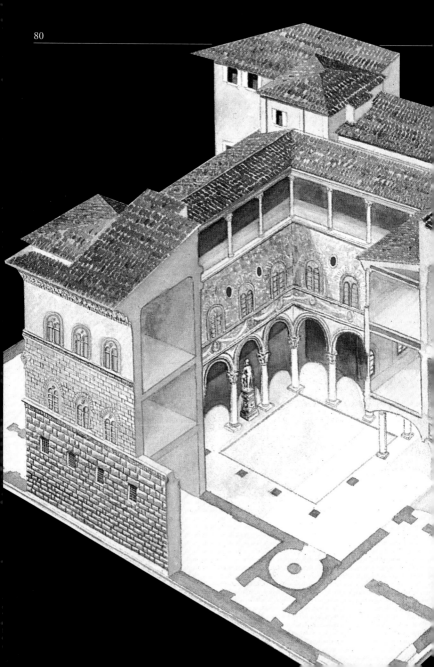

Michelozzo's Palazzo Medici (1444) was extended along the street by the Riccardi family in the 17th century. Originally it consisted of a square block around a courtyard. It bears all the characteristic features of a Florentine *palazzo*: rusticated stone façades and a square arcaded courtyard (left).

Antonio da Sangallo the Younger, Florentine by birth and by training, took the same principle to Rome for his Palazzo Farnese (1513, below). He planned three storeys of classical arcades in the courtyard, with their orders, but Michelangelo, who added the top storey, modified his design, blocking the arcades of the first storey and using windows with pilasters on the second.

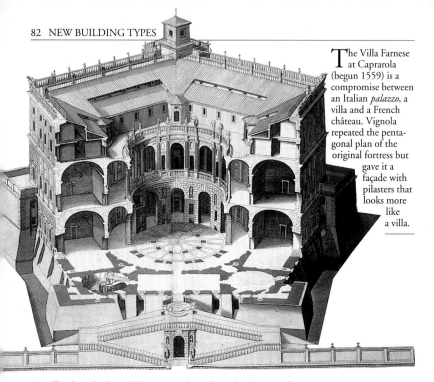

The Villa Farnese at Caprarola (begun 1559) is a compromise between an Italian *palazzo*, a villa and a French château. Vignola repeated the pentagonal plan of the original fortress but gave it a façade with pilasters that looks more like a villa.

Finally the ideal model was produced in the shape of the Palazzo Farnese. The façade with rows of pilasters reappeared briefly at the end of the 15th century in the Palazzo della Cancelleria, but was soon to be replaced by the façade introduced by Bramante, with a single order above a rusticated ground floor, which became the most widely accepted version.

The interior space was henceforward divided by right-angled walls. A new kind of staircase with straight, parallel flights divided by walls replaced the spiral staircases that had been the norm during the Middle Ages. Spiral staircases were now only used in special cases: Laurana used them in the Palazzo Ducale in Urbino, and Bramante in the Belvedere at the Vatican because, in both cases, one had to be able to ride up them on horseback (as in medieval times). At Caprarola the staircase was in a turret in the corner, which forced Vignola to use a spiral. It was Palladio's own choice to add an oval spiral in the Carità in Venice.

The villa

A new type of residence, the villa, was invented in Renaissance Italy, in response to the desire to live in the country. The earliest examples, the villas of Cosimo I de' Medici, Cafaggiolo and Careggi, designed by Michelozzo, were small castles, or manor houses dressed up as fortresses. Soon architects were tempted to try out the centralized plan on dwellings of this type. Giuliano da Sangallo designed a square, almost centralized villa at Poggio a Caiano for Lorenzo the Magnificent; Giuliano da Maiano designed a villa at Poggio Reale for the king of Naples with a quadrangular courtyard and small pavilions at each corner. Charles VIII of France and his courtiers admired it when France occupied the city in 1495. Later the villa developed by patrons choosing sites that gave panoramic views and including open loggias from which these views could be enjoyed. The most interesting examples were built in the Veneto: the Villa dei Vescovi at Luvigliano, by Falconetto, and the Villa Garzone at Ponte Casale, by Sansovino. These combine the Venetian tradition of generous exterior openings with the classical style.

The Villa Medici at Poggio a Caiano, built by Giuliano da Sangallo in about 1480, is the first example of a compact and almost symmetrical Florentine villa, tending towards a centralized plan. The painting by Giusto Utens (centre) shows the original stairs, later remodelled in the style of Pratolino (p. 65). According to Vasari, Lorenzo de' Medici (Lorenzo the Magnificent) asked Sangallo to 'make a model of what was in his mind', and this was 'so much to Lorenzo's taste' that he was told to build it. A monochrome fresco in the villa (below) depicts the scene.

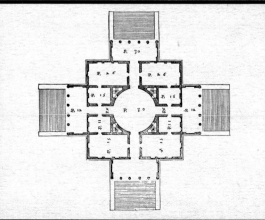

P alladio's villas have come to symbolize the Renaissance. The Villa Rotonda in Vicenza is the most celebrated, and the most perfect. It consists of a square with classical porticoes on all four sides. The interior centres on a circular *salone* in the Italian manner, that is two storeys high. The only drawback to the design is the problem of lighting the central space, which receives light only from the dome. The Villa Barbaro at Maser (overleaf) is almost as celebrated, although less for its architecture than for its site and its interior decoration. Behind the villa there is a nymphaeum with niches containing statues by Alessandro Vittoria (p. 86 bottom); inside, frescoes by Veronese with some fascinating trompe l'oeil effects (p. 87).

In Tuscany and around Rome villa design focused more on the garden than on the house. In the Veneto the flight of the Venetian aristocracy to 'terra firma' led to a tremendous growth in the number of country houses being built. Palladio transformed the genre with his skilful blend of classical inspiration and rustic charm. The Villa Capra, better known as the Villa Rotonda, in Vicenza is the most famous of all his creations; with its

Palladio first made his name as an architect in Vicenza, then as a church architect in Venice; he built many villas in the Veneto for Venetian patrons. In this portrait by Orlando Flacco (opposite) he points to the model of the *tempietto* at Maser, his final work (1580).

'Guided by a natural inclination, I gave myself up in my most early years to the study of architecture: and as it was always my opinion, that the antient Romans, as in many other things, so in building [as] well, vastly excelled all those who have been since their time, I proposed to myself Vitruvius for my master and guide, who is the only antient writer of this art, and set myself to search into the reliques of all the ancient edifices....'
Andrea Palladio
Architecture (1570)
trans. Isaac Ware, 1738

central plan and four large porticos it has the air of a classical temple, but it is unique. The most usual type of villa was less ambitious, consisting of a mansion house of simple design, dominated by a classical pronaos and surrounded by even simpler, arcaded outbuildings. The outbuildings might continue the line of the façade, as at Maser or Fanzolo, but more

A fresco of the Villa d'Este at Tivoli by Girolamo Muziano shows a vista across the gardens and fountains. The villa was designed by Pirro Ligorio for Cardinal Ippolito II d'Este around 1550 and was the first to accord overriding importance to the gardens. In fact, the fame of the Villa d'Este is based on its gardens more than its architecture.

frequently they were at right angles to frame the carriage sweep; at the Villa Badoer at Fratta Polesine the outbuildings form two concave wings.

The garden

With the emergence of the villa a new relationship grew up between a residence and its site, and as a consequence radical change took place in garden design. The traditional medieval garden was a collection of walled enclosures laid along an axis, linked by narrow doorways. This plan was soon enriched by the addition of fountains with statuary, as in the Villa Medici at Castello, and ornamental ponds. The king of Naples' villa at Poggio Reale, with its view over the Bay of Naples, its citrus groves and its lakes, had the reputation of being one of the wonders of its kind; it was probably the gardens rather than the architecture of

In this relief originally made for the *Studiolo* of the Grand Duke Francesco I de' Medici (1585, left), Giambologna depicts himself showing the duke a model of a fountain for his villa at Pratolino, visible in the background on the left.

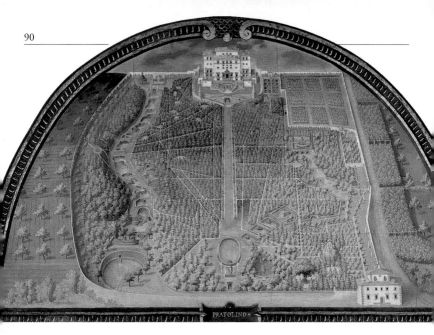

PRATOLINO

the villa that enchanted the French. Rome added classical statuary to the formula, and this soon became *de rigueur*; vistas, terracing and fountains were used to enhance the natural contours of the landscape. The Villa d'Este at Tivoli is probably the best surviving example of the style.

In the second half of the 16th century running water was added (at the Villa Lante at Bagnaia and at Caprarola); later water became an essential feature of the Baroque garden. The compartmentalized garden nevertheless remained the norm, only being challenged in the garden of Francesco I de' Medici at Pratolino, where the picturesque arrangement of little buildings and grottoes dotted all over the hillside was revolutionary. It influenced all garden design throughout the 17th century.

It was the traditional Italian garden consisting of arrangements of squares and rectangles that was copied in Renaissance dwellings outside Italy, however, as Androuet du Cerceau's writings and engravings, published in France, make clear.

The Villa Lante at Bagnaia, near Viterbo, is famous for its profusely decorated pavilions (below) as well as the beauty of its gardens.

The Spanish palace

The Italian *palazzo* could only really have influence in a Mediterranean country like Spain. Here the design could easily be adapted to local tradition by adding the classical orders to the patios of existing palaces, as in the Palacio de Miranda in Burgos or the Irish College in Salamanca; orders were sometimes added to the façade as well, as at the Palacio Vasquez de Molina in Ubeda. At La Calahorra there is even an interior courtyard constructed entirely in Genoa in the characteristic style of the late 15th century and erected in Spain by Genoese labourers; the Palacio Santa Cruz at El Viso de Marqués is a pastiche Italian *palazzo* in the style of the Palazzo Farnese, built by an emigré from Bergamo.

Pratolino, the villa designed by Buontalenti for Francesco I de' Medici, the Grand Duke of Tuscany, in 1569, was the most original of the Renaissance villas because of its gardens (opposite above). The long central perspective, the little bosquets, or woods, with fountains and statues and the waterfalls foreshadowed the characteristic features of 17th-century French gardens, for which Pratolino was the acknowledged model.

The courtyard of the Irish College in Salamanca, designed by Diego de Siloé in 1529, borrowed the Italian principle of superimposed arcades divided by piers with demi-columns.

The French château

In France and other more northern countries the Italian model was ill-suited to the climate and ill-adapted to local tradition and had little influence on urban architecture, with a couple of exceptions: the Hôtel de Ville in Paris, designed by Domenico da Cortona, and Lescot's Louvre, both commissioned by François I for very precise purposes. The French *hôtel particulier*, or urban residence, was not a continuous building; it consisted of a dwelling in a courtyard, decorated with orders of columns in the grandest cases and with a wing (usually more modest) on either side. The influence of Italy was to be seen in the design of châteaux. The fashion for centralized structures in villa design appeared in France at the beginning of the reign of François I (1515–47). The original plan for Chambord and the final building show the influence. There were smaller châteaux too, built on a square plan: La Muette at St-Germain-en-Laye, and the Duchesse d'Etampes' Challeau, both known from engravings by Androuet du Cerceau.

The original plan for Chambord (1519) consisted of a square structure, divided inside by four corridors in the form of a Greek cross; it was later integrated into a huge rectangular enclosure (above). The centralized plan of the central block reflects the influence of Tuscan villa architecture.

English country houses

England was slower than France to adopt classical principles, though the vocabulary of classicism, often introduced by Italian craftsmen, became fashionable with Henry VIII and his courtiers. The vanished palace of Nonsuch was profusely decorated with Italianate features, and they occur nearly as prominently at Hampton Court. Under Elizabeth, knowledge of Italian, French and Flemish architecture became fairly widespread (as in Longleat with its ordered façade and Wollaton with its plan based on Giuliano da Maiano's Poggio Reale).

In all these cases, however, the Renaissance elements are merely grafted on to structures that were basically medieval. It was not until Inigo Jones, in the reign

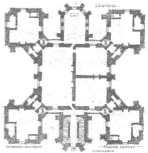

of James I, that an English architect could claim to have mastered Renaissance principles. Jones travelled in Italy; he read and assimilated Palladio; and his Banqueting House, London, and Queen's House, Greenwich, are the first really Renaissance buildings in England.

The hunting lodge at La Muette (see plan above), erected in the St-Germain forest in 1542, could be built to the centralized plan beloved of the Italians because of its small size; it was the last of such buildings in France. The Louvre, rebuilt by Lescot in 1546 (opposite below) was not arranged to any overall plan and relies entirely on its façades for effect. The rich decoration is in the French taste; the horizontal lines are punctuated by projecting bays with superimposed columns.

The castle of Spittal an der Drau in Austria, built by Italians in 1539, reproduces the Italian plan of a courtyard with loggias one on top of the other; yet, as in France, the staircase in the corner upsets the symmetry of the colonnades.

Castles in Germany

The influence of the new ideas was less pronounced
in the German-speaking areas, except where they were
promoted by Italian architects: this was the case at the
castle of Spittal an der Drau in Austria, at Juliers in the
palace that a Bolognese architect Pasqualini had built in
the citadel (destroyed during the Second World War),
at Landshut in Bavaria (in the Residenz and Schloss
Trausnitz), and in the buildings designed by Friedrich

Sustris for the Residenz in Munich. Many German
castles appear to have acquired their Renaissance features
directly from France; the new style is concerned with
ornament rather than proportion or composition.

The public square

Another invention of the architects of Renaissance
Italy was the co-ordinated public square, although it
remained something of a rarity in Renaissance times.
The first example, near the residence of the duke of
Milan in Vigevano, dates from the late 15th century.
It is a long rectangle with the cathedral on the short
side and arcaded buildings with painted façades round
the other sides. Piazzo San Marco in Venice, which
began life as a vast esplanade, came progressively
closer to this model as long uniform façades were
built in front of the residences of the Procurators
of St Mark's. It never achieved perfect symmetry

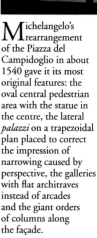

Michelangelo's
rearrangement
of the Piazza del
Campidoglio in about
1540 gave it its most
original features: the
oval central pedestrian
area with the statue in
the centre, the lateral
palazzi on a trapezoidal
plan placed to correct
the impression of
narrowing caused by
perspective, the galleries
with flat architraves
instead of arcades
and the giant orders
of columns along
the façade.

This painting by Canaletto (left) shows the Piazza San Marco as it was before Napoleon's alterations. The Procuratie Nuove extends to the right as far as the façade of Sansovino's church of San Geminiano. In his painting (below) of the Doge receiving from a fisherman the ring symbolizing his marriage to the Adriatic, Paris Bordone painted buildings with loggias above arcades, reminiscent of the Procuratie in Piazzo San Marco.

because the Procuratie Nuove, although built as continuous arcaded galleries, differed from their predecessors in the use of layered orders of columns; in addition, the short side of Piazzo San Marco, opposite the Basilica, contained a church, San Geminiano, later demolished. The Piazza del Campidoglio, redesigned by Michelangelo, is an original creation: the square itself is defined by an oval and is framed on three sides by buildings arranged in a trapezoid shape. The fourth side is open and only the palaces on either side are symmetrical. The idea of a symmetrically arranged public square was beginning to take hold. At the beginning of the 17th century such squares were built in Turin, Paris and even London (Inigo Jones' Covent Garden, 1630). Having renewed the private house, the Renaissance launched an idea that would gradually change the way cities looked.

P alladio's theatre in Vicenza (1580) commissioned by the Accademia Olimpica (hence its name, Teatro Olimpico) reproduces the classical principle of a semi-circle crowned by a colonnade and a monumental stage set, with superimposed orders of columns in front. Through the three doorways the architect (Palladio's successor Scamozzi) shows the streets of an ideal city with regular buildings in perfect perspective. The décor was supposed to represent the streets of Thebes when the theatre opened in 1585 with a production of Sophocles' *Oedipus Rex*.

A sophisticated art form presupposes an underlying culture and a set of texts. The classical era left only one treatise on architecture, by Vitruvius. The men of the Renaissance studied it, edited it, translated it, commented on it, illustrated it and were ambitious to supersede it. Renaissance architects everywhere composed their own treatises and the art of printing ensured their circulation.

CHAPTER 5
A NEW DISCIPLINE

The title page of Daniele Barbaro's edition of Vitruvius (Venice, 1556). Opposite: detail from Giovanni da Sangiovanni's *Lorenzo the Magnificent and the Arts* (1634).

With the introduction of new ideas and modes of thought during the Renaissance, architecture ceased to be simply a body of practical knowledge and became a science, requiring the mastery of several different disciplines: first and foremost drawing and perspective, but also geometry, some mathematics and a working knowledge of the language of classical architecture – the orders and proportion. The architect, conscious of his responsibilities and mindful of his art, also required some kind of basic manual on ways and means in order to keep a step ahead of his client, whom he would be required to advise. In addition, he needed to be briefed

on more general matters such as the adaptation of designs to particular sites, town planning, health and safety, economics, landscaping and technical matters such as water supply, surveying, distribution and so on. To obtain information on all these subjects, he needed books.

Editions of Vitruvius

The first book to which he would turn was Vitruvius. It may have been naive to imagine that a book written at the time of the Emperor Augustus could still be relevant, but it exemplifies the admiration and interest that people still extended towards anything from the ancient world. Vitruvius was published in Rome in 1486, with other editions following in Florence and Venice between 1495 and 1497. Besides being remote in time, the text had other drawbacks: the language, Latin with a sprinkling of Greek technical terms, was difficult, in fact virtually inaccessible to anyone not highly educated. The fact that there were no illustrations made it even more obscure. The merit of the edition published in Venice by Fra Giocondo in 1511 lay perhaps less in the correctness of the text (errors

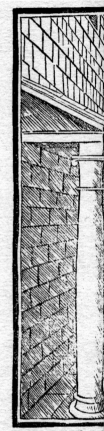

Tetraſtyla ſunt
uti litatem trabi
petum coguntu

The title page of Cesariano's translation of Vitruvius (Como, 1521, far left) bears no classical decoration; the illustration is the printer's own device.

ıbiectis fub trabibus angularibus columnis, &
firmitatem præftant, ʠ neʠ ipfæ magnum ım/
ere, neʠ ab interpenfiuis onerantur,

accumulated over centuries of copying had been
expunged) than in the illustrations, which, though
rudimentary, conveyed a basic idea; the edition went
through several reprintings almost at once. Even in
this form, however, the treatise remained more or less
inaccessible to architects because their Latin was seldom

The first illustrated
edition of Vitruvius,
by Fra Giocondo
(Venice, 1511) included
a series of simple but
expressive woodcuts.
Left: a 'tetrastyle'
courtyard surrounded
by a colonnade; the
order is not defined,
but the columns are
topped by an architrave,
not by arches. Similarly
the pediment design
(above) does not show
the mouldings in detail
but gives a clear idea of
the general structure.

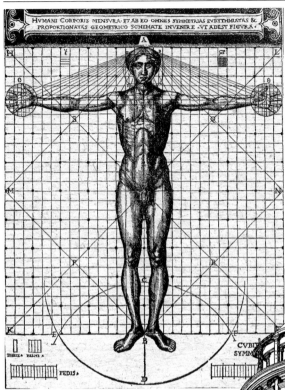

HVMANI CORPORIS MENSVRA ET AB EO OMNES SYMMETRIAS EVRYTHMIATAS & PROPORTIONATAS GEOMETRICO SCHEMATE INVENIRE VT ADEST FIGVRA

Since classical times the proportions of the human body had been the basis for the theory of proportion as set out by Vitruvius. All the illustrators had to tackle the problem. Left: Cesariano (1521) places the body in a square; the genitals are in the centre and the knees and elbows in the quarters.

adequate for the task. When Raphael decided to take a serious interest in Vitruvius he had to ask the humanist Fabio Calvo to translate it for him.

Illustrated translations

A decisive step forward was taken in Como by Cesare Cesariano, who published the first translation into Italian in 1521; his edition also had a commentary and illustrations that were much more sophisticated than the illustrations in Fra Giocondo's edition. Other translations followed, but the text remained difficult to interpret; the editions could be distinguished from one another by the quality of the accompanying commentary and the accuracy of the illustrations. The edition published in Venice by the Venetian nobleman and humanist Daniele Barbaro in the 1556 is of particular interest because the author was assisted with both by Palladio.

The book began to appear all over Europe. Jean Martin, secretary to Cardinal de Lenoncourt and a noted scholar of Italian, published the first French edition in Paris in 1547 with Fra Giocondo's wood engravings; Jean Goujon, known to history as a sculptor but also an architect, assisted in the interpretation of the text and also provided some supplementary illustrations of a far higher quality than the Venetian plates. In Nuremberg in the same year Walter Ryff, known as Rivius, published the first

ARCHITECTVRE
ou Art de bien bastir,
de Marc Vitruue Pollion Autheur
ROMAIN ANTIQVE MIS DE LATIN EN
Francoys, par Ian Martin secretaire de Mon-
seigneur le Cardinal de Lenoncourt.
POVR LE ROY TRESCHRESTIEN HENRY II.

A PARIS
AVEC PRIVILEGE DV ROY.
On les vend chez Iacques Gazeau, en la rue sainct
Iacques à l'Eseu de Cologne.
M. D. XLVII.

The first French translation of Vitruvius, by Jean Martin (1547), bears the portrait of the printer (Jean Barbé) under the title, rather than that of the author. Daniele Barbaro, assisted by Palladio (Venice 1556, below), produced a much improved commentary and illustrations extending to secondary subjects such as the measuring of water levels with a plumb-line and ruler.

Vitruvius' description of theatres gave rise to some interesting reconstructions in the illustrated editions. Cesariano was perhaps inspired by the Colosseum in this three-storeyed version with engaged columns (left).

B il Capo della Fonte,
B c la prima Mira
C d la seconda mira drieto al monte
D e la terza doue non si può condurre
D f. la quarta doue si può condurre
H g f. la condutta dell'acqua,

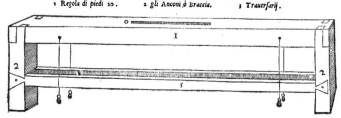

COROBATE DA LIVELLAR LE ACQVE E I PIANI.

1 Regola di piedi 20.   2 gli Anconi ò Braccia.   3 Trauersarij.

German edition with a translation of Cesariano's commentary and illustrations taken from various earlier editions. A Spanish translation by Miguel de Urrea was published in 1582.

Alberti's treatise

Vitruvius dealt with architecture from its basic principles; he proposed a theory of proportion based on harmony in music, making a clear distinction between practical problems and architecture as an art. But the projects put forward in his book belonged to the past. Even the theory of the orders, the element of classical architecture that was coming back into fashion, was set out in a confused and incomplete manner. The

Renaissance required a treatise that actually answered its needs. Alberti was already aware of this, and in about 1450 completed his *De re aedificatoria* divided into ten books, obviously aspiring to be the modern Vitruvius; his book had the drawback of being written in Latin and, in spite of its logical layout, of being limited to generalities. It was theoretical and

retrospective, using examples from classical architecture only, and was stronger on references than on solutions. At this stage of his life Alberti had built almost nothing, and he was writing for highly educated readers like himself rather than for architects. His book was a success with the former, circulating in the form of handsome manuscripts – there was one in the library of Federigo da Montefeltro, duke of Urbino and two in the library of the king of Hungary, Matthias Corvinus. It was published in 1486 and translated into Italian by Cosimo Bartoli in 1550 but it never reached the professionals. Its achievement was to make educated people aware of

This copy of Alberti's treatise (left) bears the coat of arms of Matthias Corvinus, king of Hungary, the great bibliophile and patron of the arts.

the fundamental problems of architectural design and to create an enlightened clientèle of supporters of the classical style.

The eight books of Serlio

Several architects, aware of the need for a practical manual, planned such a work, but lack of time and of theoretical background meant that their contributions usually got stuck at the early stages; there would be notes on surviving monuments, included not because they were exceptional, but simply because they had survived, then some musings on the orders during the course of which the writer would get tangled up in discrepancies between the pronouncements of Vitruvius and the evidence of classical remains. Treatises survive by Francesco di Giorgio, Giuliano da Sangallo and, from the following generation, Bernardo della Volpaia and Giovan Francesco da Sangallo, plus a number of anonymous works.

The architect who came closest to completing his projected work was Sebastiano Serlio, who was more of a theorist and teacher than a practising architect and built almost nothing.

Federigo da Montefeltro, duke of Urbino, was a man of letters as well as a soldier. While constantly enriching his library, he would accept only manuscripts, not printed books. This unusual painting (centre) shows him armed from head to foot, reading – combining both dominant features of his personality.

The chief merit of Serlio's books is their clarity. Below: an illustration from his book on geometry and perspective (1545).

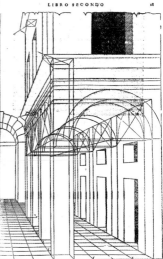

LIBRO SECONDO

Extraordina

RIO LIBRO DI ARCHI
TETTVRA DI SEBASTIA
NO SERLIO, ARCHITETTO
DEL RE CHRISTIA-
NISSIMO,

Having fled to Venice after the Sack of Rome, he conceived the idea of a great treatise in ten books, each book dealing with a different aspect of the art. He published the books in random order: first came Book IV, on the orders (Venice, 1537), then Book III on the antiquities of Rome with a few modern masterpieces to round it off (Venice, 1540). Serlio moved to France in 1540, at the invitation of François I, and settled in Fontainebleau, where he continued with his project, publishing further books in Paris in bilingual versions. Books I and II on geometry and perspective (1545), Book V on temples and religious architecture (1547), and finally, 'extraordinary' or additional to the series, a volume on monumental doorways (Lyons, 1551). Book VII, dealing with 'accidents', or the re-use of ancient buildings, was not published until after his death, in Frankfurt in 1575. The most important of all, Book VI, was about civil buildings in town and country, and was circulated in the form of two manuscripts, certainly widely read and quite influential

Serlio's plans are based on geometric designs that are highly idealized. In his *Extraordinario Libro di architettura* he publishes the design for the entrance that he had built for the residence of the Cardinal of Ferrara in Fontainebleau (below).

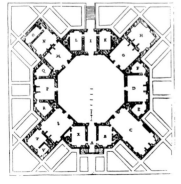

in France. These were not published until this century (1967 and 1978). An eighth book on Roman camps has never been published.

Serlio's successors

Serlio marked a transition in the literature of architecture because, instead of restricting himself (as his predecessors had) to presenting classical models on the implicit understanding that they were the only models worth following, he also published plans for buildings based on simple geometrical figures (circle, square, octagon) and their variations. These exercises in style demonstrated the ways in which Renaissance doctrine could find practical expression. In 1559 Jacques Androuet du Cerceau, who was never an architect but was an exceptional draughtsman, and was evidently familiar with Serlio's sixth book, published a *Book of Architecture* containing fifty plans for private houses to suit every purse; these were presented in increasing order of extravagance, from the simplest to the most ambitious, from the most straightforward to the most complex (or most fantastic) design. In 1582 he published a collection of thirty-eight plans for châteaux. His books had a perceptible influence on French domestic architecture, noticeable in turn-of-the-century châteaux such as Wideville or Grosbois, and this influence lasted well into the 1630s.

The sixth design in Jacques Androuet du Cerceau's final book (1582) is typical of a medium-sized French château of the latter part of the century, with its lack of an order and its stonework. The two projecting pavilions at the side and the concave treatment of the centre are reminiscent of the château at Grosbois (1597).

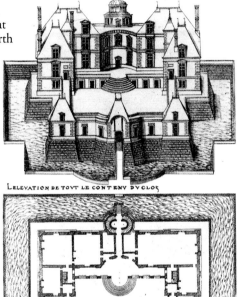

LELEVATION DE TOVT LE CONTENV DV CLOS

LE PLAN DE TOVT   LE CONTENV DV CLOS

Following Serlio's example, Palladio also published a treatise in four books, in Venice in 1570. He used classical examples to exemplify the theory of architecture, then demonstrated its practical applications using his own designs, the difference between him and Serlio being that for the most part his examples had already been built. His disciple Scamozzi followed his lead, publishing his *Idea dell'architettura universale* (Idea of Universal Architecture) in Venice in 1615.

In his *Architecture*, published in 1510, Philibert Delorme departs from the practicalities in favour of a more theoretical, Vitruvian attitude. He expounds the doctrine by working through the stages in the construction of a building, from the choice of site, bearing in mind wind and water supply, down to the details of structure and decoration. His tone is sententious, even pedagogical, and he moves from principle to principle rather than from example to example. This was only the first volume and the second, never completed, would certainly have suggested models to be imitated, probably starting with his own works; he had had engravings made of them for the purpose. If he had been able to complete his treatise it would have made him the modern Vitruvius and the French Serlio.

The title page of Palladio's treatise (1570) bears a very crowded architectural design in the Venetian style.

Manuals of the orders

In addition to these ambitious volumes, whose authors aspired to a thorough analysis of architectural theory with ideas for design and construction thrown in, the Renaissance also produced shorter, more practical manuals devoted to design and classical proportion. These were aimed at practising architects and the sheer number of them proves that they answered a need. The first was published in Spain in 1526 by Diego de Sagredo. Serlio came next, in 1537, with his *Book III: or the General Rules of Architecture*, published shortly afterwards in Antwerp in Flemish (1539), then in German and French (1542) – all were reprinted several times. In the German-speaking countries the example was followed by Walter Ryff, known as Rivius, (Nuremberg, 1547) and Hans

Blum (Zurich, 1550). It was Vignola, however, who published the manual that was to upstage them all thanks to its practical simplicity: *Regola delle cinque ordini.*

Thus the Renaissance architect had at his disposal a range of books on various subjects, from general theory to sample buildings and practical manuals. Most were richly illustrated and probably quite expensive, but the number of them in circulation and the way in which they were reprinted so quickly suggests that the price was no obstacle to their success. Few practising architects would have risen to the intellectual status of a Delorme or the archaeological knowledge of Palladio, but even if they were not true polymaths and humanists, they at least possessed a library.

The physical appearance of the great Italian masters has often been handed down to us. The portrait of Vignola (above) comes from his treatise. On the other hand, we have little information about the appearance of the French architects. The portrait of Delorme (centre) dates from the 19th century and the costume and his dignified appearance may bear some relation to the truth. His treatise (left) has a sobriety that has more to do with his milieu than with contemporary taste.

LE PREMIER TOME DE L'AR-CHITECTVRE DE PHILIBERT DE L'ORME CONSEILLIER ET AVMOnier ordinaire du Roy, & Abbé de S. Serge les Angers.

A PARIS,
Chez Federic Morel, rue S. Iean de Beauuais.
1567.
AVEC PRIVILEGE DV ROY.

In the Middle Ages cathedral builders were regarded as master masons, stoneworkers or carpenters – which indeed by training they were. The Renaissance required a more academic education of its builders, and the creation of very detailed plans.
The Greek designation 'architect' was restored: those earning the name were regarded as artists.

CHAPTER 6

A NEW PROFESSION

On one of the ceilings in the Palazzo Vecchio (right) Vasari depicts Cosimo I de' Medici surrounded by the artists in his service including, on the left, the cabinet maker Tasso, who is showing him the model of the *Mercato Nuovo*, and the sculptor Tribolo, on the right, who is showing a model for a fountain at the Villa Medici at Castello. In a fresco in the Uffizi, Pocetti depicts a gentleman visiting the studio of a military architect/engineer (left); his assistants are working on drawings and models.

The need for design

A well-trained architect, concerned with
geometry, symmetry and proportion, had to be
able to plan everything in advance. There was no
question now of building without a fixed design of
the elevation. In the Middle Ages buildings were often
constructed from a simple schema, or by the use of
the 'secret', the master-builders' trick of deducing the
elevation from the plan by the application of a simple
system of proportion based on a triangle or a square
(*ad triangulum* or *ad quadratum*). Henceforward a
whole set of blueprints had to be drawn up and for
them draughtsmanship was the essential requirement.
Drawings now became exact scale representations, with
dimensions marked and sometimes accompanied by

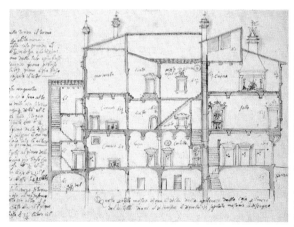

The longitudinal
section (left)
was a new kind of
representation that
allowed a closer analysis
of the structure of a
building and at the same
time the arrangement of
the interior. It requires
some extra visualizing
effort on the architect's
part, and also skill as
a draughtsman, in
suggesting reality.

drawings in different conventions: the section, to
elucidate the internal structure of a building, the
orthogonal or geometrical elevation, to show the true
proportions of the building and the perspective view, to
show the building as it would look when distorted by
the human eye. The architect ceased to be a technician
from the building site and became a designer; he
acquired his professional skills by practising drawing
rather than by working in the building trade.

Painter-architects

The first Renaissance architects received their initial training in some other art. Brunelleschi and Michelozzo, the founding fathers of Florentine architecture, were both goldsmiths by trade: this might seem incomprehensible if we did not know that, at the end of the Middle Ages, the goldsmith's trade was considered a major art form that required not only mastery of drawing and ability to make sculpture, but also a knowledge of architectural forms (if not of architecture itself), an integral part of the contemporary vocabulary of the visual arts. The Renaissance made radical changes to the language of architecture, breaking the mould; after the middle of the 15th century there were no more goldsmith architects.

As drawing and design developed, painters began to take over, even the greatest of them being tempted to try architecture. Although he never had anything built, Leonardo da Vinci pondered the subject of architecture at length, covering his sketchbooks with designs for imaginary buildings, particularly churches with a central plan and radiating chapels, which seemed to fascinate him; in his old age he designed a villa for the lieutenant of the king of France in Milan, Charles d'Amboise. Baldassare Peruzzi, the Sienese painter, is more famous for his architecture, particularly the Villa Farnesina in Rome, than for his frescoes. Raphael

A goldsmith's workshop depicted by a Florentine painter of the late 16th century (centre). In the foreground the pieces are being shown to a client, in the background they are being fashioned in the forge or on the work benches.

Leonardo da Vinci, though Florentine by birth and by training, worked at the court in Milan where centralized structures were fashionable. He too was fascinated by the theme and left many plans and sketches of churches with domes and chapels radiating from the centre (below).

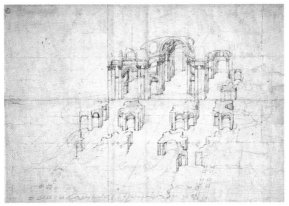

had worked with Bramante, and when Bramante died in 1514 he took over his work at St Peter's. Henceforth he devoted himself mainly to architecture, ordering a translation of Vitruvius, studying the antiquities of Rome, designing the Villa Madama and various *palazzi* (the Pandolfini in Florence, the Branconio in Rome), and drawing up plans that could replace those of Bramante for St Peter's, which had never been completely worked out. His disciple, Giulio Romano, moved to Mantua where he also became an architect and was responsible for numerous notable buildings, including the Palazzo del Tè, the Duomo and the manège in the Palazzo Ducale. Vignola was also a painter by training and appears never to have forgotten it: at Caprarola he spent his spare time painting trompe l'oeil columns. Finally Vasari, solely a painter at the outset, ended his career as the architect to the Grand Duke of Tuscany, designing the Uffizi in Florence

Bramante's first profession was painting, but he must have been introduced to architecture in Urbino where he was born. The re-building of St Peter's in Rome was his great project at the end of his life. He wanted to build a church with a huge dome, much larger than the Pantheon. His first design (p. 70) inspired Baldassare Peruzzi to draw this plan presented in axonometric form (above left) to give some idea of what the interior would have looked like. His successor Raphael (below) remained best known as a painter but practised as an architect at the end of his life. Besides St Peter's his most ambitious project was the Villa Madama built for Cardinal Giulio de' Medici (the future Pope Clement VII). In the end only the façade and the foundation of the circular court were built; the unfinished villa was painted by Hendrick Frans Van Lint in the mid-18th century (opposite above).

(at least) and the church of the Knights of St Stephen in Pisa. The most radical conversion was that of Serlio, from Bologna, a disciple of Peruzzi who had inherited his master's designs and who finally gave up painting to devote himself entirely to architecture, or, to be precise, to the theory of architecture. In Spain the architect of the Palace of Charles V in the Alhambra in Granada, Pedro Machuca, was a painter who had formerly worked in Raphael's studio in Rome.

Giorgio Vasari (below) was a painter who became a successful architect.

Sculptor-architects

Sculptors too were attracted to architecture. Michelozzo, who also trained as a goldsmith, worked with Donatello as a sculptor and became architect to Cosimo de' Medici, finally abandoning sculpture altogether. Giovanni Antonio Amadeo, a charming sculptor, became the architect of the Colleoni Chapel in Bergamo and helped introduce the centrally structured building to Lombardy, as did Piero Lombardo to Venice. Michelangelo, first and foremost a sculptor,

In this painting on one of the ceilings of the Louvre, Horace Vernet tried to illustrate the exceptional artistic production that emerged from the patronage of Pope Julius II. On his left is Michelangelo (recognizable by his broken nose) having just finished the painting of the Sistine Chapel ceiling; in front of him Bramante presents a plan of St Peter's (it is in fact that of Raphael, made after Bramante's death and known to us through an engraving by Serlio); on the right, the young Raphael with his hand on a *modello* of one of the frescoes in the *Stanze* in the Vatican. The group is highly implausible but in chronological terms would have been possible between 1508 and 1513.

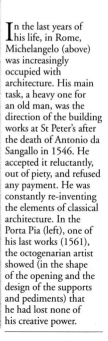

In the last years of his life, in Rome, Michelangelo (above) was increasingly occupied with architecture. His main task, a heavy one for an old man, was the direction of the building works at St Peter's after the death of Antonio da Sangallo in 1546. He accepted it reluctantly, out of piety, and refused any payment. He was constantly re-inventing the elements of classical architecture. In the Porta Pia (left), one of his last works (1561), the octogenarian artist showed (in the shape of the opening and the design of the supports and pediments) that he had lost none of his creative power.

distinguished himself in both painting and sculpture before turning to architecture. First he designed the New Sacristy in San Lorenzo in Florence, then, in Rome, accepted the huge task of St Peter's. Whatever he worked on, whether it was the vestibule of the Biblioteca Laurenziana, the courtyard of the Palazzo Farnese, the Piazza del Campidoglio, or the Porta Pia, thanks to the liberal interpretation he gave to the rules and the personal twist he gave to form and detail he always succeeded in renewing the architectural conventions.

Jacopo Sansovino, whose surname came from his sculpture teacher, became architect to the Signoria in Venice and built some of the most significant Renaissance buildings to be found there, including the Moneta, the Biblioteca Marciana and the Loggetta. His disciple, Alessandro Vittoria, designed façades for Venetian *palazzi*. In Spain, Diego de Siloé was also a sculptor by training. Architects from the building profession were few and far between during the Renaissance. The only names that occur are Mauro Codussi in Venice, Antonio da Sangallo, Sanmicheli, Palladio (who began as a stone mason) and, in France, Philibert Delorme.

The dilettantes

The new importance of drawing and theory relegated practical experience to a secondary position, to the extent that complete amateurs now became architects. The first of these dilettanti was Alberti, a Florentine nobleman and convert to humanism; not content with producing a great treatise to rival Vitruvius he embarked on the profession of architect in the service of Sigismondo Malatesta in Rimini, of Giovanni Rucellai in Florence, and of Ludovico Gonzaga in Mantua. His lack of practical competence combined with distance from

Alberti, a dilettante of genius, used the classical vocabulary in its purest form. Above: a detail of the Tempio Malatestiano in Rimini. He also wrote on painting and sculpture and left a self-portrait in bronze (below). His thin, expressive face and staring eyes convey a vivid impression of the intellectual, ever eager to understand and to learn.

the building sites forced him to rely on professionals
for the actual building: Matteo de' Pasti in Rimini,
Bernardo Rossellino in Florence, Luca Fancelli in
Mantua, and working by delegation caused its
own problems. In spite of this his buildings are
some of the most original and most beautiful
creations of the early Renaissance. Though his
talent was unique, Alberti was not the only amateur.
Alvise Corner, a Venetian nobleman living in Padua,
wrote a brief treatise in the mid-16th century and
apparently also designed some buildings, including
the theatre in his own palace. His main claim to fame,
however, was to have encouraged the painter Falconetto
to become an architect. Another amateur, the
patriarch of Aquileia, Daniele Barbaro, wrote
a learned commentary on Vitruvius and was
the patron of Palladio. Palladio himself, a simple
stone mason at the outset, seems to have owed his
advancement to the perspicacity and protection
of a gentleman of Vicenza, Giangiorgio Trissino,
for whom he designed a country house. In
France, Pierre Lescot, the architect of the
recently built Louvre, was born into the
noblesse de robe and seems to have been
a true dilettante: he apparently had to
ask the young Baptiste du Cerceau
to draw his designs for him.
Finally, in Florence, at
the end of the century,
a member of the Medici
family, Giovanni, became
a professional architect; he
took part in a competition
for a design for the façade
of Santo Stefano de'
Cavalieri in Pisa, and
it was he who provided
the plan for the enormous
Medici funerary chapel
built on the site of the
apse of the church of
San Lorenzo.

Cosimo I de' Medici, like all art-loving princes, did not neglect drawing himself. In a painting in the Palazzo Vecchio, Vasari depicted him in front of a plan of fortifications, dividers and set square in his hand, preparing for the conquest of Siena. Giovanni de' Medici, half-brother of the Grand Duke Ferdinand of Tuscany, was more than an amateur. In 1589 he received the title of Superintendent General of Fortifications, Munitions and Ordinance. In 1590 he presented a model for the completion of the façade of Florence Cathedral (opposite), produced in collaboration with Alessandro Pieroni.

Models and cabinet makers

However precise the drawings produced might be, they were never sufficient to demonstrate the building in three dimensions, particularly for clients uninstructed in their interpretation. The old practice of making a scale model in wood persisted to provide a three-dimensional view of the projected building. Competitions, beginning with the one for the dome of Florence Cathedral, often asked for a model from the candidates. While a building was under construction it was also normal practice to provide models of details so that their effect could be judged.

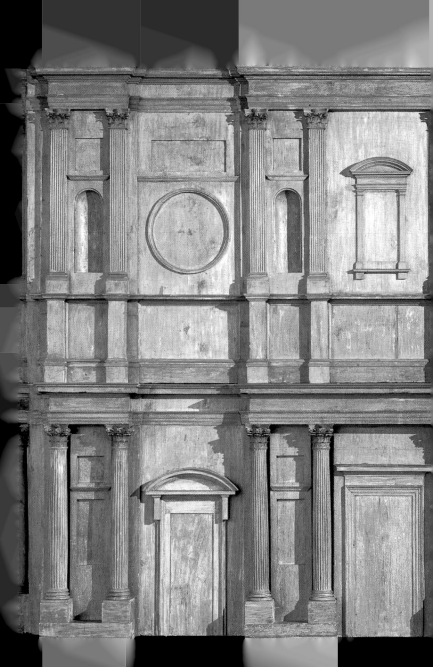

The church of San Lorenzo in Florence was the Medici parish church and had benefited from their patronage, having been rebuilt during the 15th century. The façade, however, was never finished. During the winter of 1515–6, Pope Leo X set himself to solve the problem and a number of plans were produced. Michelangelo won the commission in January 1518, but his project was never realized. It is known from drawings, and from his model in wood, which follows his plan almost exactly. The façade here is a screen that conceals rather than reveals the structure of the church. The upper corners of the second storey would have had nothing behind them.

On large building sites, like the cathedral in Pavia or St Peter's in Rome, large and very expensive models were made, so large that one could actually go inside them to judge the internal proportions. The construction of these models required the attention of a cabinet maker skilled at understanding architectural drawings and interpreting current architectural practice. As may be

In this gold relief (opposite), made by Giambologna in 1585, the artist shows Buontalenti presenting his model for the façade of Florence Cathedral. The model of half the dome of St Peter's in Rome (below) was executed on Michelangelo's instructions between 1558 and 1561; it was considerably modified by Giacomo della Porta in 1588, then by Luigi Vanvitelli in the 18th century. In the painting on the right, Passignano depicts Michelangelo presenting his model of St Peter's in Rome to Pope Paul IV. (The model shown in fact incorporates Giocomo della Porta's modifications.)

imagined, the creation of such models was a specialized skill in itself and this probably explains why in Renaissance Italy, and particularly in Florence, there were architects who had begun their training as cabinet makers. This was certainly true in the case of the first one, Antonio Manetti Ciaccheri, who started as model-maker to Brunelleschi; after Brunelleschi's death he became a specialist in domes, like his former employer. First he was commissioned to build the dome of San Lorenzo, then to continue the circular choir in the Annunziata and to design the funeral chapel for the cardinal of Portugal in San Miniato al Monte, to a centralized design. Giuliano da Sangallo, Simone del Pollaiuolo, known as Il Cronaca, and Giuliano da Maiano in Florence all had the same training, as did Domenico da Cortona, who made the first model for

Chambord and then conceived the project for the Hôtel de Ville in Paris. Antonio da Labacco, who built the model of St Peter's for Antonio da Sangallo the Younger, finally wrote his own book on architecture (Rome, 1552).

The advancement of the architect

As the profession moved away from the practical towards the theoretical, via the mastery of design, it gained progressively in status and its representatives earned a new name, derived from the Greek: architect. The designation spread through 15th-century Italy, although the name engineer persisted in Lombardy for a while. In France, the name architect arrived much later and more slowly, the function being frequently undertaken by the builders. The professional in charge continued to be called the master mason. As the two gradually separated, the name took hold.

This painting by Maso da San Friano was described in the Farnese collection as being of 'an old man teaching a young man architectural drawing'. It has been suggested that the old man is Ottavio Farnese, duke of Parma, and the young one the military engineer Francesco de' Marchi. Yet the duke's face is not recognizable; the young engineer would be behaving in an inappropriately familiar manner, and the plan on the table is of a church. It seems more likely that the picture shows an experienced architect teaching an amateur.

With a more resonant title the architect's status rose and he ceased to be identified with the builder. He became an artist and benefited from the general high profile enjoyed by the arts at the time. One proof of this is the fact that, even in Italy, architects began to sign their work in some prominent place, like painters and sculptors; for example Matteo Nuzi in Cesena (1452), Novella da San Lucano in Naples (1470), Marino Cedrini in Loreto (1476), Falconetto in Padua (1524), and Palladio at Maser (1580).

The architect thus became a personality in his own right, a cherished professional to be sought out, looked after and revered. Cosimo de' Medici treated Michelozzo as a friend; the architect accompanied his master to Venice when he was banished there in 1433, and undertook the reconstruction of the Biblioteca Camaldolensis in San Giorgio. In spite of a ban on any interments in the cathedral, the authorities of Florence Cathedral buried Brunelleschi there in 1447 in a very prominent position and decided to erect a monument to him with an effigy and a eulogy in verse, composed by the Chancellor of the Republic. Federigo da Montefeltro, duke of Urbino, prefaced his appointment of Luciano Laurana as director of works with praise to architecture and to his architect. The sought-after Sienese architect Francesco di Giorgio worked in Naples, in the Marche at Urbino, Jesi and Ancona, then at Pavia and Milan in Lombardy. In France, Philibert Delorme received the title of King's Chaplain in Ordinary from Henri II, as well as the Abbaye d'Ivry. Despite his humble background, Palladio was cultivated by the aristocratic society of the Veneto. Architecture had always been a major art form, now it became a noble one.

After 1400 it was forbidden to erect a tomb or any funeral monument inside Florence Cathedral. The decision was waived, however, in the case of the architect of the dome, Brunelleschi, who was buried in the cathedral with a

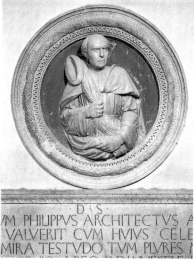

commemorative inscription in Latin and a portrait in relief carved by his disciple, Andrea Cavalcanti, called Buggiano (above).

Overleaf: on the first floor of the Farnesina, Rome, Baldassare Peruzzi exercised both his professions – painter and architect – in a trompe l'oeil architectural fresco.

DOCUMENTS

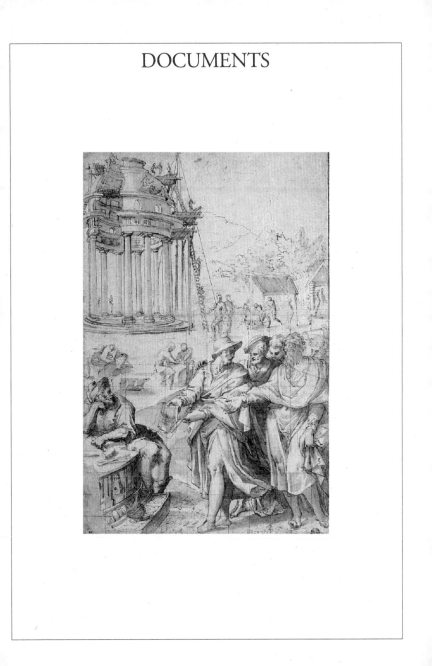

The rediscovery of antiquity and the rejection of Gothic architecture

The Renaissance condemned the style it labelled Gothic, and advocated a return to the principles and language of classical architecture. Renaissance architects studied the ruins of classical buildings closely, making drawings and publishing them: they were the first archaeologists. Their activities helped to preserve the surviving buildings.

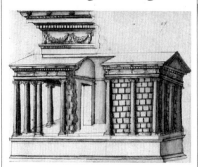

The Maison Carrée in Nîmes, drawn by G. B. Montano, in the 16th century.

Brunelleschi in Rome (1402)

While looking at the sculpture, as he had a good eye and an alert mind, he saw the way the ancients built and their proportions. As if he were enlightened concerning great things by God, he seemed to recognize quite clearly a certain order in their members and structural parts. This he noticed especially, for it looked very different from what was usual in those times. He proposed, while he was looking at the statues of the ancients, to devote no less attention to the order and method of building. And so he observed closely the supports and thrusts of the buildings, their forms, arches and inventions, according to the function they had to serve, as also their ornamental detail. In these he saw many wonders and beauties.... Brunellesco proposed to rediscover the excellent and highly ingenious building methods of the ancients and their harmonious proportions and where such proportions could be used with ease and economy without detriment to the building....

During this period in Rome he was almost continually with the sculptor Donatello. From the beginning they were in agreement concerning matters of sculpture more particularly, and to these they applied themselves continually. Donatello never opened his eyes to architecture. Filippo never told him of his interest, either because he did not see any aptitude in Donatello or perhaps because he was himself not sure of his grasp, seeing his difficulties more clearly every moment. Nevertheless, together they made rough drawings of almost all the buildings in Rome and in many places in the environs, with the measurements of the width, length and height, so far as they were able to ascertain them by judgment. In many places they had excavations done in order to see the joinings of the parts of the buildings and their nature, and whether those parts were square, polygonal or perfectly round, circular or oval, or of some other shape. And thus where they were able to estimate the height from the bases and foundations to the cornices and the roofs of the buildings, they noted the measurements on strips of parchment like those used for squaring pages, with arithmetical numbers and characters which Filippo only understood…. Because they had to dig in many places in order to investigate structures or to find buildings where some indication was discernible that some buried edifice existed, it was necessary for them to hire porters and other laborers, and this at great expense, since no one else did the thing or understood why they did it…. They were generally called the treasure-men, in the belief that they were spending treasures and seeking them.

Antonio Manetti, *Life of Brunelleschi*, trans. Elizabeth G. Holt and Creighton Gilbert In Elizabeth G. Holt (ed.), *A Documentary History of Art*, 1957

Vasari's opinion of Gothic architecture (1568)

There is another style called German, whose decorative features and proportions are very different from both the antique and the modern. Good architects today do not use it, they shun it as ugly and uncivilized. Its elements conform to no rules, and the result could be termed confusion and disorder: these buildings are so numerous that they have spread all over the world. The doorways are decorated with thin columns twisted like vine tendrils, unfit to support any weight, even the lightest. On the façades and the decorated portions accursed little niches are stacked one on top of the other with such an array of pinnacles, pyramids and foliage that it seems impossible that a collection like this should stay upright and keep its balance. It appears to be made of paper rather than stone or marble. There are so many projections, gaps, corbels, tendrils that the proportions seem all awry. Sometimes the decorative elements are piled so high around a door that the top of the door reaches the roof.

This style was created by the Goths. After demolishing the buildings of antiquity and killing all the architects in battle, they employed the survivors to raise buildings in this style: they built vaults on pointed arches, and covered the whole of Italy with these accursed constructions. The Italians, weary of these buildings, finally did away with the style altogether. May God preserve any country from this notion and from this manner of building! Such deformity compared with the beauty of our monuments means that nothing is to be gained by discussing it further.

Giorgio Vasari 'Introduction to the three arts of design', *Vite*, 1568

The decree of Anne of Montmorency, governor of Languedoc, relating to the conservation of ancient buildings in Nîmes (September 1548)

We, Anne, seigneur of Montmorency, premier baron, *connétable* and grand master of France, governor and lieutenant general of the king in Languedoc, send greetings to the judge ordinary of the town of Nîmes. As we were passing through that town, we observed large and beautiful old buildings, notable for their artifice and architecture, built by the ancients; many, indeed most, of these are not only admired today, but also are of great benefit to the art of architecture in places where proportion in architecture is studied and taught. The ancient buildings are an adornment to that town, in the Languedoc, the pride of the realm; but because some citizens of Nîmes possess houses near the aforementioned ancient edifices, to which they are daily adding new structures of a size and commodiousness to suit their owners' convenience, these ancient buildings are being concealed and gradually demolished so that before very long they will be ruined, destroyed and spoiled. For this reason, and desirous that such monuments should be conserved intact, we hereby enjoin you to forbid this in our name, and to impose grave penalties…. All owners of the ancient houses must refrain from re-building or demolishing them, nor should any buildings be erected that might cover or hide the said antiquities in any way unless the king's representatives in Lyons have first been summoned to inspect the site and to judge whether it is reasonable and appropriate to grant permission for building work to be carried out.

If any person contravenes this edict you will prosecute him and deal with the contravention. We herewith empower you and command you to proceed accordingly, and, through the authority invested in us by His Majesty the King, do order all dispensers of justice, officers and subjects of the said monarch to obey your commands in the implementation of the decree.

Louis de La Trémoille (ed.), *Revue des sociétés savantes des départements*, series 5, VIII, 1874

Palladio on architecture (1570)

After the grandeur of the Roman empire began to decline, through the continual inundations of the Barbarians, architecture, as well as the other arts and sciences, left its first beauty and eloquence, and grew gradually worse, till there scarce remained any memory of beautiful proportions, and of the ornamented manner of building, and it was reduced to the lowest pitch that could be. But, because (all human things being in a perpetual motion) it happens that they at one time rise to the summit of their perfection, and at another fall to the extremity of imperfection; architecture in the times of our fathers and grandfathers, breaking out of the darkness in which it had been for a long time as it were buried, began to shew itself once more to the world. Therefore under the pontificate of Pope Julius, Bramante, a most excellent man, and an observer of antient edifices, made most beautiful fabricks in Rome; and after him followed Michel'Angelo Buona[r]roti, Jacobi Sansovino, Baldassar da Siena, Antonio da San Gallo, Michel da San Michele, Sebastian Serlio, Georgio Vasari, Iacobo Barozzio da Vignola, and the Cavalier Lione; of whom wonderful fabricks are to be seen in Rome, in Florence, in Venice, in Milan, and in other cities of Italy. Besides which, most of them have been at the same time excellent painters and sculptors, as well as writers; and some of these are still living, together with some others whom I do not name, to avoid being tedious. But to return to our subject. Since Bramante was the first who brought good, and beautiful architecture to light, which from the time of the antients had been hid; for several reasons it seemed to me fit, that his works should have a place among the antients.

Palladio and the study of antiquity

Guided by a natural inclination, I gave myself up in my most early years to the study of architecture: and as it was always my opinion, that the antient Romans, as in many other things, so in building [as] well, vastly excelled all those who have been since their time, I proposed to myself Vitruvius for my master and guide, who is the only antient writer of this art, and set myself to search into the reliques of all the antient edifices, that, in spight of time and the cruelty of the Barbarians, yet remain; and finding them much more worthy of observation, than at first I had imagined, I began very minutely with the utmost diligence to measure every one of their parts; of which I grew at last so sollicitous an examiner, (not finding anything which was not done with reason and beautiful proportion) that I have very frequently not only travelled in different parts of Italy, but also out of it, that I might intirely, from them, comprehend what the whole had been, and reduce it into design.

Whereupon perceiving how much this common use of building was different from the observations I had made upon the said edifices, and from what I had read in Vitruvius, Leon Battista Alberti, and in other excellent writers who have been since Vitruvius, and from those also which by me have lately been practised with the utmost satisfaction and applause of those who have made use of my works; it seemed to me a thing worthy of a man, who ought not to be born for himself only, but also for the utility of others, to publish the designs of those edifices, (in collecting which, I have employed so much time, and exposed myself to so many dangers) and concisely to set down whatever in them appeared to me more worthy of consideration.

Andrea Palladio, *Architecture,* Book IV, trans. I. Ware, 1738

The new architecture

The Renaissance saw a return to the basic principles of classical architecture: regular alignments and levels, symmetry around a central entrance and proportion maintained between the parts and the whole. The classical orders provided a system of proportion and a vocabulary of ornament. The ideals were the centralized plan and the circle, the purest of geometrical forms.

The dome of the sacristy of Santo Spirito, Florence.

Proportion and harmony

Letter from Alberti to Matteo de' Pasti in Rimini, where he was in charge of the construction of the Tempio Malatestiano (18 November 1454).

With reference to your observation about Manetto [Antonio Manetti Ciaccheri] and his contention that domes should be twice as high as they are wide, I place more confidence in the builders of the great Baths and the Pantheon and all those great buildings than I do in him, and I trust reason more than I trust any person. If he persists in this opinion I should not be surprised if he is frequently mistaken. As for the pillar in my model, remember what I told you: this façade must be a work of art in its own right.... It is better to improve what has already been made and not spoil what remains to be made. You can see where the measurements and proportions of the pillars come from: if you change anything the harmony will be lost....

The law of proportion

Beauty will result from the form and correspondence of the whole, with respect to the several parts, of the parts with regard to each other, and of these again to the whole; that the structure may appear an entire and compleat body, wherein each member agrees with the other, and all necessary to compose what you intend to form.
    Andrea Palladio, *Architecture*, Book I, Chap. I, trans. Isaac Ware, 1738

Proportion and symmetry

In the length of halls I use not to exceed two squares, made from the breadth; but the nearer they come to a square, the more convenient and commendable they will be. The rooms ought to be distributed on each side of the entry and hall; and it is to be observed, that those on the right correspond with those on the left, that so the fabrick may be the same in one place as in the other, and that the walls may equally bear the burden of the roof; because if the rooms are made large in one part, and small in the other, the latter will be more fit to resist the weight, by reason of the nearness of the walls, and the former more weak, which will produce in time very great inconveniences, and ruin the whole work. The most beautiful and proportionable manners of rooms, and which succeed best, are seven, because they are either made round (tho' but seldom) or square, or their length will be the diagonal line of the square, or of a square and a third, or of one square and a half, or of one square and two thirds, or of two squares.

Andrea Palladio, *Architecture*, Book I, Chap. XXI, trans. Isaac Ware, 1738

And altho' the rooms in a house are made large, middling, and small, the windows, nevertheless, ought to be all equal in the same order or story. To take the dimensions of the said windows, I like those rooms very much whose length is two thirds more than the breadth, that is, if the breadth be eighteen foot, the length should be thirty, and I divide the breadth into four parts and a half, one I give to the breadth of the void of the window, and two to the height, adding one sixth part of the breadth more; and according to the largeness of these I make those of the other rooms.

The windows above these, that is, in the second story, ought to be a sixth part less in the height of the void, than those underneath; and in the same manner, if other windows are placed higher, they ought to diminish still a sixth part.

The windows on the right hand ought to correspond to those on the left, and those above directly over them that are below; and the doors likewise ought to be directly over one another, that the void may be over the void, and the solid upon the solid, and all face one another, so that standing at one end of the house one may see to the other, which affords both beauty and cool air in summer, besides other conveniences.

Andrea Palladio, *Architecture*, Book I, Chap. XXV, trans. Isaac Ware, 1738

The superposition of the orders

The Tuscan, Dorick, Ionick, Corinthian, and Composite, are the five orders made use of by the antients. These ought to be so disposed in a building, that the most solid may be placed undermost, as being the most proper to sustain the weight, and to give the whole edifice a more firm foundation: Therefore the Dorick must always be placed under the Ionick; the Ionick under the Corinthian; and the Corinthian under the Composite.

The Tuscan being a plain rude order, is therefore very seldom used above ground, except in villas, where one order only is employ'd. In very large buildings, as amphitheatres, and such like, where many orders are required, this, instead of the Dorick, may be placed under the Ionick.

But if you are desirous to leave out any of these orders, as, for instance, to place the Corinthian immediately over the Dorick, you may, provided you always observe to place the most strong and solid undermost, for the reasons above-mention'd.

Andrea Palladio, *Architecture*, Book I, Chap. XII, trans. Isaac Ware, 1738

The symbolism of the orders

Just as the Doric column was devised according to the dimensions and proportions of a man, and the Ionic those of a woman, so the column here [Corinthian] was devised in imitation of the slender, attractive figure of a maid. Just as young girls are slim and small and look more beautiful when they are elegantly attired, so do Corinthian columns. For they appear, or should appear, much richer and less formal, more delightful and better ornamented than the other orders. For this reason their height is more than eight times their base diameter, or nine or even more, according to where they are being placed. This is what makes them look slimmer and more delicate than the Ionic, whose height is never more than eight and a half times its base diameter, and sometimes less.

Philibert Delorme, *Architecture*,
Book VI, Chap. I, 1567

I chose the present Ionic order out of all the orders to adorn the palace [of the Tuileries] which Her Majesty the Queen, mother of the most Christian King Charles IX, is having built at this moment in Paris.... I wanted to use this order on the said palace because it is seldom used, and few people have employed it for colonnaded buildings.... The other reason is because it is feminine, and was devised according to the proportions and attire of ladies and goddesses, as the Doric was devised according to male proportions, or so the ancients have taught me. When they wanted to dedicate a temple to a particular god they would use the Doric order, and to a goddess, the Ionic.

Philibert Delorme, *Architecture*,
Book V, Chap. XXIII, 1567

Corinthian capitals.

The orders are optional, symmetry essential

It could be assumed, by those who have read what I have written about the façades of buildings concerning the disposition of the windows, that I wished to compel them to use columns or pillars [pilasters] on the outside of their buildings. This is not my intention at all. Anyone who wants to spend less money has no need of such elaboration and enrichment of the façade, and his means would anyway not be adequate to meet such great expense. It is true, however, that I require the composition and arrangement of the windows on the front of a building to comply with certain proportions and measurements, and that the arrangement of bays on one side should match that on the other, even without columns or pilasters.... In the illustration, therefore, I suggest square pillars linked by vaults to form a sort of peristyle with a gallery above it, the whole without columns, pedestals, capitals or cornices; to demonstrate that a well-trained and experienced architect can create an elegant building without great expense. Such a building can be just as pleasing as others that are far more opulent.

Philibert Delorme, *Architecture*,
Book I, Chap. XVII, 1567

The centralized plan and the advantages of the circle

Temples are made round, quadrangular, of six, eight, and more sides; all which terminate in the capacity of a circle, in the form of a cross, and of many other forms and figures, according to the various inventions of men, which, when they are done with beautiful and suitable proportions, and distinguished by elegant and ornamented architecture, they deserve to be praised. But the most beautiful, and most regular forms, and from which the others receive their measures, are the round, and the quadrangular; and therefore Vitruvius only mentions these two, and shews us how they are to be comparted, as shall be inserted when the compartment of temples comes to be treated of. In temples that are not round, one ought carefully to observe, that all the angles be equal, let the temple be of four, of six, or of more sides and angles.

Thus we read, that the antients in building their temples endeavoured to observe the decorum, in which consists the most beautiful part of architecture. And therefore we also, that have no false gods, in order to observe the decorum concerning the form of temples, must chuse the most perfect, and most excellent. And since, the round one is such, because it is the only one amongst all the figures that is simple, uniform, equal, strong, and capacious, let us make our temples round. For which purposes this figure is particularly fit, because it being inclosed by one termination only, in which is to be found neither beginning nor end, nor are they to be distinguished one from the other; but having its parts similar one to another, and all participating of the figure of the whole; in a word the extream being found in all its parts, equally distant from the middle, it is exceeding proper to demonstrate the infinite essence, the uniformity, and the justice of God.

Besides which, it cannot be denied, but that strength and perpetuity, is more sought after in churches, than in all other fabricks; since they are dedicated to the omnipotent and supream God; and that in them are preserved the most celebrated and most memorable things of the city. Hence, and for this reason also, it ought to be said, that the round figure, in which there is never an angle, is particularly suited to temples.

Temples ought also to be very capacious, that many people may there be able to assist at divine service. And among all the figures that are terminated by an equal circumference, none is more capacious than the round. Those churches also are very laudable, that are made in the form of a cross, which have their entrance in the part that represents the foot of the cross, and opposite to which should be the principal altar, and the choir; and in the two branches, that are extended from either side like arms, two other entrances, or two other altars; because that being fashioned in the form of the cross, they represent to the eyes of the beholders that wood from which depended our salvation. And of this form, I have made the church of San Giorgio Maggiore at Venice.

Andrea Palladio, *Architecture*, Book IV, Chap. II, trans. Isaac Ware, 1738

The design and the model

The academic view of architecture taken in the Renaissance required more detailed plans than in the past. Various methods of representing a building were employed, including the plan, the orthogonal elevation, the perspective view and the section. Wooden models were used to monitor progress and to present the project to clients.

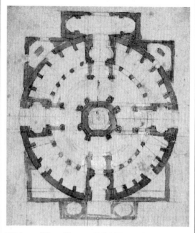

Plan of San Giovanni dei Fiorentini, Rome, by Michelangelo.

The plan, elevation and section according to Raphael (1519)

In this clumsily expressed letter, Raphael recommends that the elevation and section should be drawn directly above the plan in order that they should conform to the same scale: he emphasizes the need for a geometrical drawing to show the measurements accurately, and rejects the perspective view, which he regards as deceptive.

Because the manner of drawing employed by an architect is different from that of a painter, I shall describe the way that seems to me appropriate for the communication of the measurements and the location of all the elements of a building without error. Thus the method of drawing a building proper to the architect consists of three parts, the first being the plan or two-dimensional layout, the second the exterior view with its ornaments and the third the interior section, also with its ornaments.

The plan is the drawing that shows the flat layout of the building plot, that is the foundations of the whole building at ground level. Although this will be raised above the ground when it is built, it must be drawn flat on the ground, and made in such a way that the section of the masonry, is shown as flat and parallel at every level of the building. In order to do this one must calculate the axis perpendicular to the base...thus all the walls will be plumb above the foundations. This drawing is called the plan [*pianta*], as I said, because it illustrates the total extent of the foundations of the building as the sole [*pianta*] of the foot covers the area that is the foundation of the whole body.

Once the plan has been drawn up and divided into its constituent parts, with their dimensions, whether it is round or square or any other shape, a line should be drawn (always using the same scale) the width of the base of the whole building; in the exact middle of this line a perpendicular line should be drawn with two right angles at the base. This will mark the exact centre of the

Design by Antonio da Sangallo the Younger for a circular temple; it clearly shows the two types of representation described by Raphael: the plan (above) and the elevation (top).

building. At either end of the base line
two parallel perpendicular lines should
be drawn, to the exact height of the
building – these will show the height
of the building. Between these two lines
at either end giving the height, the
measurements will be inscribed of the
columns, mullions, windows and other
details shown on the drawing of the
façade in the plan of the building;
and the lines of these columns, piers
[pilasters or mullions?], openings etc.
must always be drawn parallel to the
lines at either end. Next the levels
of the bases of the columns, capitals,
architraves, windows, friezes, cornices
etc will be indicated horizontally. These
lines will be drawn parallel to the base
plan of the building. In these drawings
there should be no foreshortening at
the extremities (even if the building is
round or square) to show both sides,
because the architect cannot obtain
measurements from perspective
drawings; it is essential in his art that the
measurements be absolutely exact and all
the lines parallel, conveying the reality
and not the semblance. If the measurements of circular forms are sometimes
foreshortened these can at once be
checked against the ground plan. The
ones that are foreshortened on the plan
– vaults, arches, triangles – will be in
perfect proportion on the geometrical
drawings. This is why the exact measurements – *palmi*, feet, inches and even the
tiniest lines – must always be to hand.

The third part of the drawing is, as
we have said, what is called the interior
face with its ornaments, and this part is
no less vital than the other two. Like the
other two it is constructed by means of
parallel lines drawn from the ground
plan (as was the elevation). It shows half
the interior of the building as if it had
been cut in two: it shows the interior

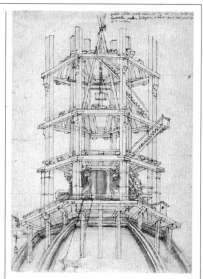

Drawing by Girolamo da Cremona
showing the building of Florence
Cathedral.

courtyard, the relationship of the level
of the exterior and interior cornices, the
height of the windows, doors, arches
and vaults and whether the latter are
round, pointed or of any other form.
In conclusion, with these three orders
or rather methods of drawing, all the
separate parts of a building, interior and
exterior, can be examined in detail.

Extract from a letter to Leo X
in *Raffaello nei documenti*,
ed. Vincenzo Golzio, 1936

**Philibert Delorme's views on the
advantages and disadvantages of plans
and models (1567)**

Chapter X

The architect must make manifest
his intentions by means of plans and

elevations and other means, in particular by a life-like scale model of the whole building.

I could easily write a whole volume on the faults I have observed in buildings, and not only those belonging to kings, princes and noble lords, but also those of the less exalted, simply because the project had not been sufficiently carefully planned, nor had adequate accurate models been made to give a clear idea of what was to be built; the models too are often faulty and misleading and are frequently con- structed by ignorant folk. Almost every day we observe the provision of pictures and designs by people who for the most part could not lay their hands to it at all without the help of artists. The latter are very adept at depicting light and shade, at applying tints, washes, shading and colouring, but have no skill at all at layout and measurement. To my way of thinking architects and builders who do this are like parrots who can speak well, but who do not know what they are saying, nor what the outcome of their promises should be, which of course is that it should be done well.... I have seen other grave errors being committed when master masons have described to artists what they want done, and the said painters, required to depict what has been described, proclaim themselves forthwith great architects, as we mentioned previously, and are presump- tuous enough to undertake building works – as indeed do joiners and sculptors on occasion. Simply because they have heard masons talking, or have watched them measuring a façade, or have made a model under the guidance of an architect or master mason, they are convinced that henceforth they are the worlds' finest and have earned a great reputation as an architect.

Chapter XI

There should not be one single model of a projected building but several, each concerned with a different part of the edifice and with the convenience and comforts that part will provide.

I agree that a model should be made of the whole building that you wish to erect, provided that additional models are then made of the separate parts of the building, in order that the ornaments and measurements of each part should be known. You should therefore make models of the vestibule, the portico, the peristyles and portals, the stoves and bathrooms, staircases, chapels, fireplaces, dormers and other parts, where necessary, and where there are to be embellishments these should be shown....

When your models are made, it will be a simple matter for a man of intelligence and sound judgment to estimate if the enterprise is feasible or not, if it is as you wish it to be, if it is well adapted to the purposes for which it is to be built, and if the ornament is correct and appropriate. Certainly one of the chief functions of a model is that it shows whether the architect is sufficiently competent to undertake a full-scale building; the model will demonstrate how well he understands his art. It will also give an idea of the cost of the project, whether it is acceptable or whether it exceeds the amount you wish to spend.

Philibert Delorme
Architecture, 1567

The architect

In the 15th century the Renaissance began paying architects a new kind of respect. The formulation of a precise doctrine opened the profession of architecture to people with no previous building experience. Outside Italy the new language sometimes annoyed professionals and encouraged abuses.

T he architect Giuliano da Sangallo.

Brunelleschi's funeral honours (18 February 1447)

The noble, wise masters of the fabric of Florence Cathedral, as well as Battista Arnolfini and Piero di Cardinale Rucellai, have been given the responsibility (by decision of the Arte della Lana) of organizing the obsequies of a man noted for his eloquence and talent, Filippo Brunelleschi, citizen of Florence, who for many years was in charge of the dome and lantern of the cathedral; by his hard work and skill he constructed the great dome without any centering, as witnessed by the masters of the fabric and the citizens as well. To honour his mortal remains and to render unto him eternal glory, they desire to take the following steps, unanimously adopted, agreed upon and organized: Filippo's body, which was first buried in the *campanile*, should be removed from that site and placed within the church, below the paving, precisely at that spot where the principal officials take the oath, almost in the centre, and he should be buried very deep. And, when the paving has been replaced, a marble slab bearing the inscription *Filippus Architector* should appear, surmounted by an arch. On the wall nearest to the place where his body will be interred, in the first lunette, should be placed a monument of stone and marble on which should be carved an effigy in his likeness, along with some of the devices that he invented or used during the completion of the dome. And to his honour and eternal glory should be dedicated some lines of verse celebrating his diligence and his skill as an architect, the verses to be composed by the celebrated Carlo Marsuppini, Chancellor of Florence: these to be placed on the front of the monument.

It has been declared that the cathedral workshop will supply all the marble required and workmen to carry out the work, and that Brunelleschi's heirs should be responsible for all the other expenses of the funeral.

The Renaissance comes to England

John Shute, who described himself as a 'painter and architect', went to Italy some time around 1550, read Vitruvius and all the modern writers he could find, and published his First and Chief Grounds of Architecture *in 1563. The first introduction to the subject in English (and in fact the first recorded use of the word 'architecture'), it is a highly practical book, describing and illustrating the forms, proportions and uses of the classical orders. At this date there were virtually no examples of the style to be seen in England, except on a small scale in a few tomb monuments. Shute emphasizes that it is a style that has to be learned, with a grammar and vocabulary of its own, just like Latin, a style for the new scholar-architect, not the old artisan-builder.*

I thought it therefore good to set out and commit to writing in our native language part of those things which (both by great labour and travail at the first for my private commodity I searched out, and for my own pleasure out of divers as well Latin and Italian as French and Dutch writers) I have diligently gathered. As also passed many countries and regions to see, both in Rome amongst the antiquities and in the most notable places of Italy, where are most excellent buildings. And intending to write of architecture or buildings, I though it best neither with the lightest or least profitable part thereof to begin, nor altogether after the most slender sort to handle that which I purposed to entreat upon. I have therefore taken my first entrance into the writing of this art at the five antique pillars or columns, commonly named of the places and persons partly where and of whom they were invented, and partly of their virtues and properties of those that they were likened unto, which pillars' names are there as followeth: Tuscana, Dorica, Ionica, Corinthia and Composita. The treatise of these pillars, as it hath in it most delectation and pleasure in the beauty and comeliness of the workmanship appertaining to them, so though at the beginning it be mingled with a little asperity and, as it were, bitterness (for the difficulty and hardness wherewith as both principles and also other things of any excellency at the first are customed to be, it is somewhat umbrous), yet it is both so necessary and profitable, that neither without it any man may attain to any estimable part of the rest of this science, and with it as by a clue of thread or plain pathway a man may most easily pierce and lightly pass over the most dark and unknown corners of the whole process thereof. But to speak of the worthiness of this part of architecture, it seemeth almost altogether superfluous, wherefore taking there to suffice in the past to be said, I will now show what trade and order I do follow in the declaration of the measures, proportions and garnishments of these before-mentioned pillars. For so much therefore as in teaching of all arts, three things are chiefly to be considered: that is to say, diligence in giving the precepts, aptness in choosing plain and evident examples, and last of all, practice and experience of the teacher.

John Shute
*The First and Chief Grounds
of Architecture*, 1563

Amateur architects

One begins to see fabricks that have something good in them...also in many other places of less fame, particularly in Vicenza, a city of no very large circumference, but full of most noble intellects, and abounding sufficiently with riches; and where I had first an opportunity to practise what I now publish for common utility, where a great number of very beautiful fabricks are to be seen, and where there have been many gentlemen very studious in this art, who, for their nobility and excellent learning, are not unworthy to be numbered among the most illustrious; as Signor Giovan Giorgio Trissino, the splendor of our times; the Counts Marc'Antonio and Adriano De Thieni, brothers; Signor Antenore Pagello, Knight; and besides these, who are passed to a better life, having eternized their memory in their beautiful and most adorned fabricks, there is now Signor Fabio Monza, intelligent in a great many things; Signor Elio De Belli, son of Signor Valerio, famous for the artifice of camei's and engraving in crystal; Signor Antonio Francesco Oliviera, who, besides the knowledge of many sciences, is an architect, and an excellent poet, as he has shewn in his *Alemana*, a poem in heroick verse, and in a fabrick of his at Boschi di Nanto, a place in the Vicentine; and lastly, (to omit many more, who might very deservedly be placed in the same rank) Signor Valerio Barbarano, a most diligent observer of all that belongs to this profession.

Andrea Palladio, Preface, *Architecture* (1570), trans. Isaac Ware, 1738

The courtyard in the Palazzo Ducale, Urbino, home of Federigo da Montefeltro, duke of Urbino.

Architects' jargon

One day Pihourt, a mason of Rennes, saddled up his mare, and, with straw on his boots, a robe roughly tied with string around the waist and his hat askew, rode to Chateaubriant where a fine château was to be built. When he heard the great craftsmen, who had been summoned from all over France talking of nothing but frontispieces, pedestals, obelisks, columns, capitals, friezes, cornices, dados, none of which he had ever heard

of in his life before, he was dumbfounded. When it was his turn to speak…he said to them (paying them back in their own currency) that in his opinion the building should be built well and competently, with an adequate palison, as required. When he had had his say, all those present deemed him a great man, to be listened to with great care on this important matter that they were unable fully to comprehend; they reckoned that

he must know a thing or two. Before he went away, the victorious builder warned that he could stay no longer but that the set of the sleeves could never be correct without him and the equipolation of his heteroclites. The assembled company were amazed by him (they had no idea what he was talking about), and this gave rise to the saying: 'as resolute as Pihourt and his heteroclites'.

Noël du Fail, *Contes et discours d'Eutrapel*, 1585

Federigo da Montefeltro appoints Luciano Laurana as architect of the Palazzo Ducale, Urbino

Having searched everywhere, especially in Tuscany, the fount of architects, without finding anyone who really understood these matters and was an expert in his craft; and having eventually heard by reputation and then seen and known by experience how learned and knowledgeable in this art is the excellent master Luciano, bearer of this letter; and having deliberated about building in our city of Urbino a fine and worthy palace fitting the rank and glorious fame of our ancestors; we have chosen and designated the said master Luciano as deviser and head of the masters to work on this enterprise, both the masons and stoneworkers, carpenters and blacksmiths and all other persons of whatever standing who might take part in the said work…giving the said master Luciano full power, discretion and authority to dismiss and send away any master or workman present on the site who does not please him or fails to give satisfaction, and to engage others….

Letter of Federigo da Montefeltro
10 June 1468

ARCHITECTS AND TREATISES	PROJECTS AND COMPLETED BUILDINGS	BUILDINGS IN EUROPE
		Dates refer to the beginning of building work
1377 • Birth of Brunelleschi		
	1420 • Project for the dome of Florence Cathedral by Brunelleschi	
1404 • Birth of Alberti		
	1421 • Façade of the Ospedale degli Innocenti, Florence, by Brunelleschi • The Old Sacristy of San Lorenzo, Florence, by Brunelleschi	
1439 • Birth of Francesco di Giorgio	**1429** • Pazzi Chapel in Santa Croce, Florence, by Brunelleschi	
1444 • Birth of Bramante	**1444** • Palazzo Medici, Florence, by Michelozzo • Plans for the choir of the Annunziata, Florence, by Michelozzo • Santo Spirito, Florence, by Brunelleschi	
1446 • Death of Brunelleschi		
1447 • Birth of Biagio Rossetti	**1451** • Palazzo Pitti, Florence	
	1454 • Refacing of the Tempio Malatestiano, Rimini, by Alberti	
	1455 • Palazzo Rucellai, Florence, by Alberti	
	1468 • San Michele in Isola, Venice, by Mauro Codussi	
	1470 • Colleoni Chapel, Bergamo, by Amadeo • Courtyard of the Palazzo Venezia, Rome, by Francesco dal Borgo • Sanctuary of San Giobbe, Venice, by Piero Lombardo	
1472 • Death of Alberti	**1472** • Sant' Andrea, Mantua, by Alberti	
1475 • Birth of Michelangelo	**1476** • Courtyard of the Palazzo Ducale, Urbino, by Francesco di Giorgio?	
	1478 • Santa Maria presso San Satiro, Milan, by Bramante	
	c. 1480 • Villa Medici, Poggio a Caiano, by G. da Sangallo	

Florence Cathedral

ARCHITECTS AND TREATISES	PROJECTS AND COMPLETED BUILDINGS	BUILDINGS IN EUROPE
1483 • Birth of Raphael • Birth of Antonio da Sangallo the Younger	**1480** • Santa Maria della Pace, Rome	
	1481 • Santa Maria de' Miracoli, Venice, by Piero Lombardo	
	1483 • Palazzo della Cancelleria, Rome, by Baccio Pontelli?	
	1484 • Santa Maria di Calcinaio, Cortona, by Francesco di Giorgio	
1486 • Publication of Alberti's treatise, *De re aedificatoria* • Publication of Vitruvius in Rome	**1485** • Palazzo della Comune, Jesi, by Francesco di Giorgio • Santa Maria delle Carceri, Prato, by Giuliano da Sangallo	
	1487 • Villa Poggio Reale, Naples, by Giuliano da Maiano	
	**1488** • The Incoronata, Lodi, by Giovanni Battagio • Sacristy of Santo Spirito, Florence, by Giuliano da Sangallo • Santa Maria della Passione, Milan, by Giovanni Battagio	
	1489 • Palazzo Strozzi, Florence, by Giuliano da Sangallo and Il Cronaca	
	1490 • Pavia Cathedral • Santa Maria della Croce, Crema, by Giovanni Battagio	
	1492 • Palazzo dei Diamanti, Ferrara, by Biagio Rossetti • Sanctuary of Santa Maria delle Grazie, Milan, by Bramante • Piazza of Vigevano	
	1494 • San Francesco, Ferrara, by Biagio Rossetti	
c. 1499 • Birth of Giulio Romano		

ARCHITECTS AND TREATISES	PROJECTS AND COMPLETED BUILDINGS	BUILDINGS IN EUROPE
	1497 • San Giovanni Crisostomo, Venice, by Mauro Coducci	**1500** • Louis XII wing at Blois
	1502 • *Tempietto* of San Pietro in Montorio, Rome, by Bramante	**1501** • Château at Gaillon
	1505 • First plan for St Peter's, Rome, by Bramante • Plan for the courtyard of the Belvedere at the Vatican by Bramante	
	1506 • New plan for St Peter's, Rome, by Bramante	
1508 • Birth of Palladio	**1508** • Santa Maria della Consolazione, Todi, by Bramante?	
1511 • Publication of first illustrated edition of Vitruvius by Fra Giocondo Birth of Vasari	**1509** • Villa Chigi, known as Villa Farnesina, Rome, by Baldassare Peruzzi	**1509** • Courtyard at La Calahorra by Michele Carlone
	1513 • Plan for the Palazzo Farnese, Rome, by Antonio da Sangallo the Younger	
1514 • Death of Bramante	**c. 1514** • Left wing of the San Damasio courtyard in the Vatican by Bramante	
1516 • Death of Biagio Rossetti	**1515** • Santa Maria di Piazza, Busto Arsizio • Villa Madama, Rome, by Raphael	**1515** • François I wing at Blois • Château at Chenonceaux
	1518 Madonna di San Biagio, Montepulciano, by Antonio da Sangallo the Elder	**1519** • Original plan for Chambord
1520 • Death of Raphael	**1520** • New Sacristy in San Lorenzo, Florence, by Michelangelo	
1521 • First Italian translation of Vitruvius by Cesare Cesariano	**1524** • Loggia of the Palazzo Corner, Padua, by Falconetto	**1526** • Work resumed at Chambord on the definitive plan
	1525 • Palazzo del Tè, Mantua, by Giulio Romano	**1527** • Château de Madrid in the Bois de Boulogne
1526 • Publication of *Medidas del Romano* by Diego de Sagredo	**1526** • Entrance to the Biblioteca Laurenziana, Florence, by Michelangelo	• Plans for the Palace of Charles V, Granada, by Pedro Machuca

ARCHITECTS AND TREATISES	PROJECTS AND COMPLETED BUILDINGS	BUILDINGS IN EUROPE
		1528 • Oval Court at Fontainebleau • Plans for Granada Cathedral by Diego de Siloé
	1530 • Odeon of the Palazzo Corner, Padua, by Alvise Corner?	**1529** • Courtyard of the Irish College, Salamanca, by Diego de Siloé
	c. 1530 • Palazzo Bevilacqua and Pompei, Verona, by Sanmicheli	**1532** • Hôtel de Ville, Paris, by Domenico da Cortona
	c. 1533 • Palazzo Canossa, Verona, by Sanmicheli	
	1536 • The Moneta, Venice, by Jacopo Sansovino	**1536** • San Salvador, Ubeda, by Diego de Siloé
Château de Madrid in the Bois de Boulogne (destroyed)	**1537** • The Biblioteca San Marco, Venice, by Jacopo Sansovino	**1537** • Italian wings of the Residenz, Landshut
	1539 • Model by Antonio da Sangallo the Younger for St Peter's, Rome	**1539** • Châteaux at Ecouen and St-Germain-en-Laye
	1540 • Michelangelo's plans for the Piazza del Campidoglio, Rome	**1541** • The Lonja in Saragossa
	1542 • Plan for the Palazzo Thiene, Vicenza, by Palladio	**1542** • Château de La Muette, St-Germain-en-Laye • Hospital of St John the Baptist, Toledo, by Covarrubias
		1543 • The Alcazar, Toledo, by Covarrubias
1546 • Death of Giulio Romano and of Antonio da Sangallo the Younger • Michelangelo made director of building works at St Peter's, Rome	**1545** • Mantua Cathedral by Giulio Romano Palazzo Corner, known as Ca' Grande, Venice, by Sansovino	**1545** • Château at Ancy-le-Franc by Serlio • Palacio de Miranda, Burgos

Château de Madrid in the Bois de Boulogne (destroyed)

ARCHITECTS AND TREATISES

BUILDINGS IN EUROPE

1547
• First French translation of Vitruvius by Jean Martin
• First German translation of Vitruvius by Rivius

The dome of St Peter's, Rome

1550
• Edition of Vitruvius with commentary by Daniele Barbaro
• First edition of Vasari's *Vite*

1559
• *Livre de Architecture* by Jacques Androuet du Cerceau

1562
• Publication of Vignola's *Regola delle cinque ordini*

1564
• Death of Michelangelo

1549
• Basilica (Palazzo Comunale), Vicenza, by Palladio

1550
• Palazzo Chiericati, Vicenza, by Palladio
• Villa d'Este, Tivoli, by Pirro Ligorio

1551
• Villa Giulia, Rome, by Vignola

1552
• Santa Maria di Carignano, Genoa, by Galeazzo Alessi

1553
• Palazzo Marino, Milan, by Galeazzo Alessi

1556
• Palazzo Grimani on the Grand Canal, Venice, by Sanmicheli

1559
• Completion of the Villa Barbaro, Maser, by Palladio
• The Madonna di Campagna, Verona, by Sanmicheli
• Villa Farnese, Caprarola, by Vignola

1560
• Cloister of the convent of the Carità, Venice, by Palladio
• Courtyard of the Palazzo Pitti, Florence, by Ammannati
• Uffizi, Florence, by Vasari

1561
• Porta Pia, Rome, by Michelangelo

1564
• Collegio Borromeo, Pavia, by Pellegrino Tibaldi

1547
• Château at Anet by Philibert Delorme

1548
• Ducal palace, Juliers, by Pasqualini
• Jaén Cathedral, by Vandelvira

1549
• Lescot's plans for the Louvre

1550
• Château de La Tour d'Aigues

c. 1557
• Petit Château at Chantilly by Bullant

1559
• Plans for the Escorial by Juan Bautista de Toledo

c. 1560
• Ott-Heinrichsbau, Heidelberg
• Reliquary chapel in Sigüenza Cathedral

1560
• Hospital de la Sagrada Sangre, Seville, by Hernan Ruiz

1562
• Palacio Vazquez de Molina, Ubeda

1564
• Palacio Santa Cruz, El Viso del Marqués, by G. B. Castello
• The Tuileries by Philibert Delorme

ARCHITECTS AND TREATISES	PROJECTS AND COMPLETED BUILDINGS	BUILDINGS IN EUROPE
1567 • Publication of Philibert Delorme's *Architecture*	**1566** • San Giorgio Maggiore, Venice, by Palladio • Villa Capra, known as Villa Rotonda, and Palazzo Valmarana, Vicenza, by Palladio	**1568** • Fontainebleau (Aile de la Belle Cheminée) by Primaticcio
	1568 • The Gesù, Rome, by Vignola	**1573** • Façades of Schloss Trausnitz, Landshut, by Friedrich Sustris
1570 • Death of Philibert Delorme • Publication of Palladio's *Architecture*	**1569** • San Fedele, Milan, by Pellegrino Tibaldi • Villa Medici at Pratolino	**1574** • The Escorial by Herrera
1574 • Death of Vasari	**1571** • Façade of the Gesù in Rome, by Giacomo della Porta	**1576** • The gallery at Chenonceaux by Bullant
1576 • *Le premier volume des plus excellents bastiments de France* by Jacques Androuet du Cerceau	**1576** • The Redentore, Venice, by Palladio	**1580** • Zamosc (new town) by Bernardo Morando
1577 • Publication of *Instructiones fabricae et suppellectilis ecclesiasticae* by St Charles (Borromeo)	**1580** • Chapel at Maser and Teatro Olimpico, Vicenza, by Palladio	**1581** • Grotto courtyard in the Residenz, Munich, by Friedrich Sustris
1580 • Death of Palladio		**1583** • Jesuit church in Munich by Friedrich Sustris
	1586 • Procuratie Nuove, Venice, by Scamozzi	**1587** • Façade of the Palacio de la Cancillería, Granada
	1588 • Dome of St Peter's, Rome, by Giacomo della Porta	**1595** • Grande Galerie of the Louvre
The façade of the Gesù, Rome		**1597** • Château at Grosbois
		1601 • Frederick V wing, Heidelberg
1615 • Publication of Scamozzi's *L'Idea dell'architettura universale*		**1605 and 1607** • Place des Vosges and Place Dauphine, Paris

FURTHER READING

GENERAL

Ackerman, James S., *The Villa: Form and Ideology in Country Houses*, 1990

Burckhardt, Jacob, *The Architecture of the Italian Renaissance*, translated by James Palmer and edited by Peter Murray, 1987

Hersey, George Leonard, *Pythagorean Palaces: Magic and Architecture in the Italian Renaissance*, 1976

Lowry, Bates, *Renaissance Architecture*, 1962

Murray, Linda, *The High Renaissance and Mannerism*, 1986

Murray, Peter, and Linda Murray, *The Art of the Renaissance*, 1963

Pevsner, Nikolaus, *An Outline of European Architecture*, 1963

The Renaissance from Brunelleschi to Michelangelo: The Representation of Architecture, edited by Henry A. Millon, 1994

Thomson, David, *Renaissance Architecture: Critics, Patrons, Luxury*, 1993

MONOGRAPHS ON ITALIAN ARCHITECTS

Ackerman, James S., *Palladio*, 1966

—, *The Architecture of Michelangelo*, 1970

Argan, Giulio Carlo, and Bruno Contardi, *Michelangelo: Architect*, translated by Marion L. Grayson, 1993

Battisti, Eugenio, *Brunelleschi*, 1981

Bruschi, Arnaldo, *Bramante*, 1973

Hartt, Frederick, *Giulio Romano*, 2 vols., 1958

Howard, Deborah, *Jacopo Sansovino. Architecture and Patronage in Renaissance Venice*, 1975

Kent, William Winthrop, *The Life and Works of Baldassare Peruzzi of Siena*, 1925

Leon Battista Alberti, edited by Joseph Rykwert and Anne Engel, 1994

Manetti, Antonio, *The Life of Brunelleschi*, edited by Howard Saalman, 1970

Murray, Linda, *Michelangelo*, 1980

Tolnay, C. de, *Michelangelo*, 5 vols., 1943–60

ON ENGLAND

Summerson, John Newenham, *Architecture in Britain, 1530 to 1830*, 1953

—, *Inigo Jones*, 1966

ON FRANCE

Blunt, Anthony, *Art and Architecture in France, 1500–1700*, 1953

—, *Philibert Delorme*, 1958

ON GERMANY

Hitchcock, Henry Russell, *German Renaissance Architecture*, 1981

ON ITALY

Anderson, William James, *The Architecture of the Renaissance in Italy*, 1927

Hartt, Frederick, *History of Italian Renaissance Art: Painting, Sculpture, Architecture*, 1994

Heydenreich, Ludwig H., and Wolfgang Lotz, *Architecture in Italy 1400–1600*, translated by Mary Hottinger, 1974

Lotz, Wolfgang, *Studies in Italian Renaissance Architecture*, 1977

McAndrew, John, *Venetian Architecture of the Early Renaissance*, 1980

Murray, Peter, *The Architecture of the Italian Renaissance*, 1986

The Thames and Hudson Dictionary of the Italian Renaissance, edited by John R. Hale, 1995

Wittkower, Rudolf, *Architectural Principles in the Age of Humanism*, 1952

ON SPAIN

Bevan, Bernard, *History of Spanish Architecture*, 1938

Kubler, George, *Building the Escorial*, 1982

—, and Martín Sebastían Soria, *Art and Architecture in Spain and Portugal and their American Dominions, 1500 to 1800*, 1959

Rosenthal, Earl E., *The Cathedral of Granada: A Study in the Spanish Renaissance*, 1961

—, *The Palace of Charles V in Granada*, 1985

TEXTS

Alberti, Leon Battista, *On the Art of Building in Ten Books*, translated by Joseph Rykwert, Neil Leach, Robert Tavernor, 1988

Filarete, Antonio Averlino, *Treatise on Architecture*, translated by John R. Spencer, 2 vols., 1965

Palladio, Andrea, *I quattro libri dell'architettura*, 1570

—, *The Four Books of Andrea Palladio's Architecture*, translated by Isaac Ware, 1738

Scamozzi, Vincenzo, *L'idea dell'architettura universale*, 1615

Serlio, Sebastiano, *The Five Books of Architecture*, 1982

Vasari, Giorgio, *Lives of the Most Eminent Painters, Sculptors and Architects*, translated by G. du D. De Vere, 10 vols., 1912–5

Vignola, Giacomo Barozzi da, *I quattro libri dell'architettura*, 1562, first English edition, 1669

—, *Regola delle cinque ordini de architettura*, 1562

LIST OF ILLUSTRATIONS

INDEX

PHOTO CREDITS

Artephot/Oronoz, Paris 27, 34l, 62–3, 91. Artephot/Bencini 28r, 35, 41b, 78. Artephot/Nimatallah 65, 83.
Dr Wilfried Bahnmüller, Geretsried-Gelting 93b. Bibliothèque Nationale de France, Paris 13, 14–5, 20br, 26–7, 45b, 77, 130, 136, 148–9. Bildarchiv Preussischer Kulturbesitz, Berlin 71b. Arch. Phot Paris/©Spadem 1995, Paris 30, 33a, 34r, 46–7, 50. Dagli Orti, Paris 15, 16, 25, 54, 55, 60, 76–7, 82, 82–3, 88, 98, 104–5, 108–9, 112–3, 116–7. Electa 68–9a, 68–9b, 104, 119a. Ecole Nationale Supérieure des Beaux-Arts, Paris 22–3, 39, 40–1, 42, 42–3, 44–5, 99, 100, 100–1, 101, 102a, 102b, 103a, 103b, 105, 106a, 106r, 107, 108, 109a, 109b. Fitzwilliam Museum, University of Cambridge 115a. Franco Maria Ricci back cover, 1–9. Gallimard spine, 24, 63a. Gallimard/Dorling Kindersley 29. Giraudon, Vanves 94–5, 110, 113, 121. Giraudon/Alinari/Anderson 30–1, 48–9, 151. Giraudon/ Alinari 76, 146–7. Giraudon/Hanfstaegl 142. Lauros-Giraudon 36b. Magnum/Erich Lessing, Paris 37, 52–3, 53, 61, 86a, 86b, 87, 96–7, 128. Museum of Fine Arts, Boston, front cover, 38. Réunion des Musées Nationaux, Paris 12, 16–7, 18–9, 46r, 92b, 118r, 119b, 129. Roger-Viollet, Paris 92a, 144–5, 150. The John and Mable Ringling Museum of Art, Sarasota, Florida 56–7. Scala, Florence 11, 14, 17a, 17b, 20bl, 26, 28l, 32–3, 33cr, 40, 46l, 48, 49, 51, 52, 58a, 58b, 59, 60–1, 63b, 64, 66, 67a, 67b, 70–1, 72, 72–3, 78–9, 79, 84–5a, 88–9, 89, 90a, 90b, 95, 111, 112, 114a, 114b, 115b, 118l, 120, 120–1, 122–3, 124a, 124b, 125, 126, 127, 133, 134, 138, 139, 140, 159.